Simple Treats

a wheat-free, dairy-free guide to scrumptious baked goods

by Ellen Abraham

Book Publishing Company
Summertown, Tennessee

Cover design: Warren Jefferson
Interior design: Gwynelle Dismukes
Photography: Warren Jefferson
Editor: Carol Lorente

Published in the United States by
Book Publishing Company
P.O. Box 99
Summertown, TN 38483
1-888-260-8458

Printed in Canada

ISBN 1-57067-137-0

08 07 06 05 04 03   6 5 4 3 2 1

Calculations for the nutritional analyses in this book are based on the average number of servings listed with the recipes and the average amount of an ingredient if a range is called for. Calculations are rounded up to the nearest gram. If two options for an ingredient are listed, the first one is used. Not included are fat used for frying (unless the amount is specified in the recipe), optional ingredients, or serving suggestions.

Abraham, Ellen, 1972-
  Simple treats / by Ellen Abraham.
     p. cm.
Includes index.
  ISBN 1-57067-137-0
  1. Baking. I. Title.

TX763.A22 2003
641.8'15--dc21

                       2003001040

Table of Contents

Acknowledgements 4

Foreword 6

Introduction 8

A Word About Baking, Vegan-Style 11

A Word About the Ingredients 14

A Simple Treats Glossary 17

 ## Muffins and Breads 19

Cookies 45

Cakes 73

Crèmes, Frostings, and Glazes 99

The Well-Stocked Vegan Baking Pantry 116

Tools for the Baker 118

Sources for Ingredients & Equipment 121

Index 123

Acknowledgements

First I would love to thank everyone at the Natural Gourmet who helped shape my love of food above and beyond my wildest dreams. To Lisa for your extraordinary precision; to Susan Baldassano for your encouragement and brave choices and your incredible ease in your approach to food; to Melanie Ferrera for your passions and for seeing and helping me cultivate my own; to Roberta Atti Johnson for helping me find myself; to Haranth for all of your creativity; to Jenny Matthou for making me understand; to Cheryl Perry with your amazing sensibility, beauty, and the true understanding of soul-food; to Jerri, who helped inspire and encourage; and to all of my classmates who participated in the journey—thank you, thank you, thank you. And in most sincerity, to Anne Marie Colbin, who definitively shaped my world with a pragmatic, realistic, holistic, spiritual, and beautifully honest approach to whole foods.

I'd like to thank my publishers, Cynthia and Bob Holzapfel at Book Publishing Company, for taking on this project willingly and in earnest; to my editor Carol Wiley Lorente, who helped me through the sometimes rough process of editing; and to all who were involved in the process.

To Jill, my sister, for testing and tasting and retesting and retasting—without her, these recipes wouldn't exist... for her unconditional loyalty, support, and her unbelievable sense of business and attention to detail... above all, for her love, which far exceeds anything I've ever known. Thank you, Bean.

To Karen, my sister, who single-handedly bought every Simple Treat within a five-mile radius of her home and made all of the stores keep the shelves stocked on a regular basis... for her unconditional love and her conscious love... Karen, you are my role model.

To Mom and Dad, who have given me everything I could have ever needed and asked for... both of you have given me the mind, endurance, will, respect, love, and loyalty that I could never second-guess. To Dad with your support and your unbelievable mind; to Mom with your style, grace, and beauty in your approach to everything you do in life... I will always honor both of you and love you with all of my heart.

To friends along the way—to Koa at Real Food Daily, who made me love barley flour; to Matthew and Dave, for giving me reasons to write; to Linda B. for always making me feel better than better; to Susan Wheeler, who helped get Simple Treats up and baking; to all at ABCO Metals, who always supported us; to Richard and crew at Orleans Whole Foods, who showed support for Simple Treats from go; to Bikram and your amazing yoga and for making me question HUMANITY; to Pangea, Vegan Essentials, PETA, Farm Sanctuary, WSPA, and all who support our veggie, animal, and human loving community.

 I dedicate this to Jill, Karen, Dad, and Momma for making all of this possible.

Foreword

Some people go vegan because they care about their health. Vegans live about 10 years longer than average and are far less likely to struggle with a host of ailments. Good reason I guess—but not enough to sway me. I try to take reasonable care of my body, but as one who enjoys occasional junk food and the not-so-occasional martini, I would never be called a health nut.

Some do it for the environment. Growing grain to feed animals rather than directly feeding people is incredibly inefficient—a waste of resources. Speaking of waste—contaminants from animal farms pollute our soil, flood our waterways, and wreak havoc on the Earth.

I did it for the animals. I never felt comfortable eating them. Then one look at the battery cages in which egg-laying chickens are crammed so tight they can hardly move, and my ability to enjoy eggs was gone. A little thinking about dairy cows bellowing for babies that had been carted off to veal crates, and I was off dairy, too.

Could one enjoy life without eggs and dairy? I knew there were vegan desserts out there—that healthy fruity stuff. And I had tasted fat-free cookies that seemed to have been made from boxes of granola—box included. Resigned to a future without anything rich and scrumptious, I was ready to make the supreme sacrifice.

Then Ellen and Jill sent me some brownies. Oh, my Lord! The best I had ever tasted. Not the best vegan brownies—the best brownies. Period. I tried a few more of their simple treats, and all my images of self-sacrifice for The Cause were destroyed. This was going to be embarrassingly easy!

I have ordered those brownies as birthday gifts and tokens of appreciation for friends and some great activists. The news that Simple Treats is releasing a cookbook so that I can occasionally make them myself is wonderful.

Thank you, Ellen and Jill. I can't wait to start baking!

Karen Dawn, Founder of DawnWatch
an animal advocacy media watch
based at www.DawnWatch.com

"If you have men who will exclude any of God's creatures from the shelter of compassion and pity, you will have men who will deal likewise with their fellow men."
— St. Francis of Assisi

Once upon a time...

...there was a vegan girl who was desperately in search of some vegan treats. She looked high and low, scouring the local markets, farmers' markets, and specialty stores everywhere, but to no avail. One day she ventured into a supermarket health food store with her close companion, Sweet Tooth. "There's got to be a vegan treat in here for us to eat," she said, and so they began to look. Finally, they came upon a vegan treat, but to their dismay, it was made with refined sugar. Then she found an organic treat, but it contained dairy products. "Hmmm," she sighed, but she continued to look. At last she found a vegan treat. It was made with some organic ingredients, but when she looked more closely, she discovered it was made with a bad, hydrogenated fat called margarine. She and Sweet Tooth became very frustrated with their search and left the market discouraged. They sat down under a tree. Together as they sat, they began to dream of the perfect sweet treat, how it would taste, and what it would be made of, as if their thoughts could bring it to life.

"First," Sweet Tooth exclaimed, "It has to be real—no tofu and no egg replacer, just simple and wholesome."

The young vegan girl added, "And it has to be made with organic ingredients, to help save the earth and ourselves. And, of course, it has to be friendly to everyone, including the animals, so no dairy, eggs, or anything that may have come from them." They both agreed.

Then the girl shouted excitedly, "It should be free of refined sugar and refined flour; it should even be wheat-free!" So it was agreed upon: Only natural sweeteners and whole-grain, wheat-free flours were to be used in these dream-baked goods.

Now they were both thrilled. They could sense that the treats were coming closer to becoming a reality. "What would they taste like?" Sweet Tooth asked, and they looked at each other for a long time. "They would taste—why, they would taste real," replied the vegan girl.

They went back to the market and bought all of the best organic ingredients—barley flour, maple syrup, and rolled oats, to name a few—and they went home and baked. And they baked, and they baked. Hours turned into days, days turned into weeks, and weeks turned into years. Finally, after all of their hard work, they came up with the simplest, sweetest, most enjoyable vegan treats ever made. Vegans and nonvegans alike agreed and gobbled them up.

Finally content, the vegan girl and Sweet Tooth lived, baked and ate happily ever after.

That is their story.

These are their recipes.

"In a gentle way, you can shake the world."
— Mahatma Gandhi

Simple Treats

—the name of this book and the name of the bakery my sister Jill Abraham, a.k.a. Sweet Tooth, and I, a.k.a. Vegan Girl, own in Eastham, Massachusetts—was created for those who are interested in making a change, through diet, through thoughtful food choices, and through action. Whether you or someone you know has food allergies or other food restrictions, or if you have consciously chosen to eat well, you are a part of that change. Although I can't say the recipes need organic ingredients to be tasty or turn out correctly, I encourage you to use them; they really do make a difference.

All of the recipes in this book have been diligently thought out, tried, and tested to be true. Each has been created with love and thoughtfulness and the knowledge and satisfaction that people of like minds would be able to experience the joy of creating them in their own homes.

Here's to the dream of healthful, organic, vegan, wheat–free, refined sugar–free, amazing *Simple Treats*.

Ellen Abraham

"Be the change you wish to see
in the world"
– Mahatma Gandhi

A Word About Baking, Vegan-Style

The following recipes are fun, simple, and easy to follow, but they do require a few points of attention:

Vegan baked products do not rely on eggs for leavening. Because the primary leaveners in these vegan recipes are baking soda and baking powder, it is important that, once the wet ingredients have been mixed into the dry ingredients, the batter is poured or the cookies are formed and baked immediately. This is because once the ingredients are mixed, the baking soda and baking powder will begin to react chemically with the other ingredients, and, in turn, create the desired rising effect in each recipe: mini-explosions. These reactions last only a short time, so you want to get the recipe into the oven before the batter runs out of these explosions and loses its ability to rise properly.

About cookies: You will see in the recipes that we say to bake the cookies for a few minutes and then rotate the cookie sheets to ensure even baking. This is because most ovens have "hot spots" and as a result, some cookies could overbake or even burn before the other cookies have baked through.

We bake all of our cookies on parchment-lined cookie sheets or on nonstick cookie sheet liners called Silpats. Silpats are washable and reusable. (See Sources, pages 121-22, to purchase Silpats; parchment paper is available in most supermarkets.) Cookies don't stick to parchment or to Silpats—they literally slide off the pan—and cleanup is virtually a quick and easy rinse-and-dry affair. It also means you can forgo oiling the baking sheets. However, if you don't have parchment paper or Silpats, use a generously oiled cooking sheet to prevent sticking.

About cakes: We also instruct you to rotate cake pans about two-thirds of the way through the baking time to account for hot spots in the oven. In addition, it is very important not to disturb the cake in the first 20 to 25 minutes of baking time because the cake could fall, sink, or collapse. Do not open the oven door or tread heavily in the kitchen—the batter needs uninterrupted baking time to be all it can be. When the "setting" time has past and the cake has cleared its most fragile stage, it becomes relatively sturdy. At this point, the pans should be rotated.

I recommend baking cakes with a baking sheet on the rack below to avoid having to clean the oven any time cake batter spills or drips over the sides of the pans.

About muffins and breads: Muffins and breads are also prone to the same type of collapse as cakes, so the general cake rules apply to them as well (see above). Here are some additional concerns when baking muffins and breads.

- More often than not, they contain ingredients such as fruits, dried fruits, nuts, etc. Some ingredients, especially fruit, bring with them additional liquid. A recipe may call for juice of half a lemon, but that amount could vary from fruit to fruit.
- In general, muffin and bread batters are stiffer than cake batters. In some recipes, I call for the addition of 1 or 2 tablespoons of soymilk if the batter is too stiff. Use your own judgment. You want the batter stiff enough not to spill over the sides of your muffin pans, but loose enough for the leaveners to work. This may take some trial and error. Like cakes, bake them with a baking sheet on the rack below to avoid having to clean the oven.

Loaf pans are called for in the bread recipes, but feel free to use an 8 x 8-inch cake pan, 8-inch round cake pan or 1- or 1½-quart casserole if you'd like. This will decrease the initial baking time from 30–40 minutes to 25–30 minutes; then rotate the pans and bake 5 to 10 minutes more.

Other suggestions:

- Whole wheat pastry flour can be subsituted for barley flour in all of the recipes.

- Sifting isn't absolutely necessary but it ensures there won't be clumps of flour or salt in the batter. In instances where sifting is not necessary, the recipe will say so, but sifting never hurts. In some recipes, such as topping mixtures, sifting is always desirable.

- Maple sugar, Sucanat, and date sugar can be used interchangeably without any significant flavor alterations. It is best to use your preference. Maple sugar adds wonderful flavor but it is very expensive, as is date sugar. Sucanat is the most cost-efficient, lending a wonderful molasses-like flavor, and is what we use at Simple Treats Bakery.

- Likewise, canola, safflower, and sunflower oils are all relatively mild-tasting oils that can be used interchangeably.

- To make the baking process flow, first preheat the oven. Then gather all of the ingredients called for in the recipe and all of the pans, bowls, measuring cups, spoons, whisks, oven mitts, et al, that you will need to prepare the recipe. French cooks call this mise en place (MEEZ ahn plahs); it saves valuable time that might otherwise be wasted searching the kitchen for supplies while your precious batter awaits.

A Word About the Ingredients

Welcome to the wonderful world of Simple Treats. The Simple Treats cookbook was created to get the word out that incredibly delicious sweets can be made vegan-style. Not only do our cookies, cakes, muffins, and breads contain no animal products, but they also use no strange substitutions. Plus, there are no baking hoops to jump through, so they're also simple to make. Whether you are taking the bold step into veganism or simply looking for alternatives to the traditional sugary, high-fat, or dairy-laden desserts, this book is designed for those who enjoy their sweets. Our experience has been that, if you love cookies, muffins and other great desserts, you will enjoy these recipes. They are a collection of our tried and true delicacies and all of our best-sellers at Simple Treats Bakery on Cape Cod in Eastham, Massachusetts. They are straightforward and easy to follow, and you don't have to be a professional to make them.

But before we get started, let's talk about what we believe are important aspects of the Simple Treats philosophy: vegan, organic, non-GMO, sugar- and wheat-free baking.

What is Vegan-Style? Vegans do not eat or use any products derived from animals, including dairy products, honey, and eggs, in our baked goods. Most vegans do not wear any animal products like leather, suede, or fur, nor do they use products that have been tested on animals.

A word about genetically altered foods. Genetically modified organisms—called GMOs—infiltrated our food supply long before the public was made aware of their presence. GMOs are foods that have been genetically manipulated to enhance or add a quality to the food. The effects GMOs will have on the environment and on the health of all beings is still uncertain. There has been much protest as of late about genetically engineered foods. Much of Europe has banned these "super foods," but in the United States, GMOs are present in more than 60 percent of the conventional foods we consume; that means we can be 60 percent certain that crops raised nonorganically have been genetically altered. GMOs have already proven to cause serious problems in the ecosystems in which they are used. These "Franken-foods" can be especially problematic for vegans and vegetarians, because they may have been "crossed" with animal genes. And anyone with food allergies may find themselves suddenly experiencing allergic reactions, unaware that the heretofore safe food now contains genes from foods to which they are allergic. And there's no label on the product to let us know.

What is Organic? Organic foods are grown without the use of synthetic pesticides, herbicides, fungicides, toxic sludge, or genetically modified organisms. The chemicals used to keep "pests" off crops may cause severe damage to our person and to the ecosystem. While we continue to be concerned about the spraying of these chemicals on crops, the chemicals have found their way inside the crops, so the same chemicals we wash off our vegetables and fruits are now a part of them. Organic farming is better for the environment and for our health. It causes less pollution, produces healthful foods, and it doesn't mess with the delicate balance of nature's ecosystem.

Wheat-free. Every one of these recipes is wheat-free. We do use wheat on occasion in the bakery, but we find that whole-grain barley flour gives our treats just the right flavor and texture. As it turns out, wheat is a highly allergenic food. Barley also is easier on the digestive system. We proudly offer this wheat-free alternative in these recipes, but feel free to substitute whole wheat pastry flour for barley flour in the recipes.

Refined Sugar–Free. Because of the imbalances white sugar causes in the body, we won't use it. We prefer to use all-natural, gentler sweeteners. In addition, due to the way white sugar is processed, there is a chance it may not even be vegan (it is filtered through charred animal bones), so we rely on the more natural, obviously vegan alternatives. These include:

Liquid sweeteners:

Agave: A sweet syrup derived from the blue agave cactus. (Yes, the same plant that brings you tequila.) Tastes similar to honey.

Barley malt syrup: A sweet syrup with a strong malt flavor, derived from sprouted barley. Where barley malt syrup is called for, you may use half maple syrup.

Maple syrup: The familiar syrup from the sugar maple tree.

Rice syrup: Derived from rice, it's less sweet than the other liquid sweeteners. Where rice syrup is called for, you may use half maple syrup.

Dry sweeteners:

Use these sweeteners interchangeably.

Date sugar: Ground, dried dates.

Maple sugar: Dried, powdered maple syrup.

Sucanat: Dehydrated sugarcane juice.

Read more about these sweeteners in the Glossary on the next pages.

A Simple Treats Glossary

Agar (also called agar agar): A flavorless seaweed used as a thickening agent. It helps to bind and set like gelatin. Available as a powder, solid bars, or flakes in natural food stores. Our recipes call for agar flakes.

Agave: A syrup derived from the blue agave cactus, a plant native to Mexico used in making tequila. Tastes similar to honey but is not an animal product. Agave can be found in most natural food stores and through mail order.

Barley flour: A whole-grain flour made from barley.

Barley malt: A syrup made from sprouted barley. It is less sweet than maple syrup and has a strong fermented malt flavor.

Brown rice syrup: A syrup made from sprouted brown rice. Less sweet than maple syrup. Has a slight caramel flavor.

Carob: Also known as St. John's Bread. Carob is derived from a pod; when ground, the powder has a similar flavor and appearance as cocoa. Unlike cocoa, it is naturally sweet, caffeine-free, and contains several vitamins and minerals. Also available roasted, which is more flavorful than plain, and is the better choice for desserts and baked goods.

Coffee substitutes: Powder or granules with the flavor of coffee, usually made from grain. Roma and Pero are commonly known brands; Oskri is a new, organic brand.

Date sugar: A sweetener consisting of ground, dried dates. Can be substituted for other granulated sugars. It also adds moistness to baked goods.

Kudzu: The starchy root of the kudzu plant, used as a thickening agent. Commonly sold in small rock-like pieces, it is an unrefined ingredient used much like cornstarch or arrowroot.

Lemon powder: Dehydrated lemon juice, available by mail order. (See Sources, pages 121-22.)

Maple syrup: Syrup made from boiling down the sap of the sugar maple tree. Conventional syrup may be processed with nonvegan agents such as detergents or lard, so use organic, kosher syrup.

Maple sugar, powder, and crystals: Dried, powdered form of maple syrup. Can be substituted for Sucanat (below) and date sugar (above). Available in some natural food stores and through mail order.

Soymilk: A beverage made by cooking crushed, soaked soybeans and water. Sold in natural food stores and most supermarkets in aseptic packages and in the refrigerated dairy section.

Sucanat: Dehydrated sugarcane juice. Has a mild, sweet, molasses flavor. Can be substituted for maple sugar and date sugar.

Tahini: A paste made from ground toasted or raw sesame seeds. Although not as thick as peanut butter, the flavor is reminiscent. Toasted tahini will be more flavorful.

Zest: The very outer skin of citrus fruit. Avoid the white pith underneath, which has a bitter flavor.

Note: These ingredients are available in most supermarkets, natural food stores, or by mail order. (See Sources, pages 121-22.)

Muffins and Breads

Blueberry Muffins

☆ ☆

Blueberry muffins are always a treat to wake up to and this recipe is simple and quick. Fresh blueberries are always at their best later in the summer months, but frozen berries work wonderfully all year round.

Topping:

    2 teaspoons maple sugar, Sucanat, or
        date sugar
    1 teaspoon barley flour

Muffins:

    ½ cup canola, safflower, or sunflower oil
    ½ cup maple syrup
    1¼ cups soymilk
    2 teaspoons apple cider vinegar
    1 teaspoon vanilla
    ½ cup Sucanat, date sugar, or maple
        sugar
    3½ cups barley flour
    2 teaspoons baking soda
    2 teaspoons baking powder
    ½ teaspoon grated nutmeg
    1 teaspoon salt
    2 cups whole fresh or frozen, unthawed,
        blueberries, divided

    Note: If using frozen blueberries, do not
    thaw before adding to the batter.
    Previously frozen berries will turn the
    batter blue.

Preheat the oven to 350°F. Oil a 12-cup muffin pan or line it with unbleached paper liners and set aside. In a small bowl, mix the sugar and flour for the topping; set aside.

Mix the oil, syrup, soymilk, vinegar, and vanilla in another small bowl. In a separate, larger bowl, place the Sucanat; sift the flour, baking soda, baking powder, nutmeg, and salt into the Sucanat. (Sifting isn't absolutely necessary, but it ensures there won't be clumps of flour or salt in the batter.) Whisk the wet ingredients into the dry ingredients. Do not overwork the batter. If the batter seems very stiff, add 1 teaspoon soymilk. Fold in 1½ cups of the blueberries. Do not overmix or batter will turn blue. Finish mixing with a spatula to scrape the sides of the bowl.

Spoon the batter into the prepared pan. Sprinkle the muffins with the topping mixture and the remaining ½ cup blueberries, placing 2 or 3 whole blueberries on top of each muffin.

Bake for 20 minutes and rotate the pan a half turn to ensure even baking. Bake 5 to 6 minutes more or until a knife inserted in the center of a muffin comes out clean. Let cool for about 15 minutes. Remove from the pan and let cool completely on a wire rack.

For Blueberry–Oat Bran Muffins

Use 3 cups barley flour and 1 cup oat bran.

 Per muffin: Calories 290, Protein 5 g, Fat 10 g, Carbohydrate 47 g, Fiber 7 g, Sodium 455 mg

Raspberry Muffins

☆ ☆

One of our customers, a chiropractor, drives two hours just to pick up some of these muffins before heading off to work. A hint of ground cloves lends these muffins a uniquely different flavor. Fresh, organic raspberries aren't always easy to find, so feel free to use frozen berries.

Topping:

2 teaspoons maple sugar, Sucanat, or date sugar

1 teaspoon barley flour

Muffins:

½ cup canola, safflower, or sunflower oil

½ cup maple syrup

¾ cup soymilk

2 teaspoons apple cider vinegar

2 teaspoons raspberry extract

1 teaspoon vanilla

½ cup Sucanat, date sugar, or maple sugar

3 cups barley flour

2 teaspoons baking soda

2 teaspoons baking powder

¼ teaspoon ground cloves

1 teaspoon salt

1½ cups chopped raspberries

12 whole fresh or frozen, unthawed, raspberries

Preheat the oven to 350°F. Oil a 12-cup muffin pan or line it with unbleached paper liners and set aside. In a small bowl, mix the sugar and flour for the topping; set aside.

Mix the oil, syrup, soymilk, vinegar, raspberry extract, and vanilla in another small bowl.

In a separate, larger bowl, place the Sucanat; sift the flour, baking soda, baking powder, cloves, and salt into the Sucanat. (Sifting isn't absolutely necessary, but it ensures there won't be clumps of flour or salt in the batter.) Whisk the wet ingredients into the dry ingredients. Do not overwork the batter. If the batter seems very stiff, add 1 teaspoon soymilk. Finish mixing with a spatula to scrape the sides of the bowl. Fold in the chopped raspberries.

Spoon the batter into the prepared pan. Sprinkle with the topping mixture and place 1 whole raspberry on top of each muffin.

Bake for 20 minutes and rotate the pan a half turn to ensure even baking. Bake 5 to 6 minutes more or until a knife inserted in the center of a muffin comes out clean. Let cool for about 15 minutes. Remove from the pan and let cool completely on a wire rack.

Note: If using frozen raspberries, do not thaw; to chop, pulse frozen berries in a food processor or blender. If using fresh raspberries, chop in a food processor or blender or by hand.

Per muffin: Calories 266, Protein 4 g, Fat 10 g, Carbohydrate 42 g, Fiber 6 g, Sodium 452 mg

Apple-Walnut Muffins

☆ ☆

Makes 1 dozen muffins

These muffins taste like old-fashioned donuts—without the guilt. Dusted with Cinnamon-Maple Sugar, they are a wonderful treat.

Cinnamon-Maple Sugar:

½ cup barley flour

3 tablespoons maple sugar, Sucanat, or date sugar

1 teaspoon ground cinnamon

¼ teaspoon salt

Muffins:

½ cup canola, safflower, or sunflower oil

½ cup maple syrup

¾ cup soymilk

2 teaspoons apple cider vinegar

1 teaspoon vanilla

½ cup chopped walnuts

½ cup Sucanat, date sugar, or maple sugar

3½ cups barley flour

2 teaspoons baking soda

2 teaspoons baking powder

2 teaspoons ground cinnamon

¼ teaspoon grated nutmeg

1 teaspoon salt

4 apples, peeled and finely chopped

Preheat the oven to 350°F. Oil a 12-cup muffin pan or line it with unbleached paper liners and set aside. In a small bowl, mix the Cinnamon-Maple Sugar ingredients; set aside.

Mix the oil, syrup, soymilk, vinegar, and vanilla in another small bowl.

In a separate, larger bowl, place the walnuts and the Sucanat; sift the flour, baking soda, baking powder, cinnamon, nutmeg, and salt into the walnut mixture. (Sifting isn't absolutely necessary, but it ensures there won't be clumps of flour or salt in the batter.) Whisk the wet ingredients into the dry ingredients. Do not overwork the batter. If the batter seems very stiff, add 1 teaspoon soymilk. Finish mixing with a spatula to scrape the sides of the bowl. Fold in the chopped apples.

Spoon the batter into the prepared pan. Sprinkle with the Cinnamon-Maple Sugar.

Bake for 20 minutes and rotate the pan a half turn to ensure even baking. Bake 5 to 6 minutes more or until a knife inserted in the center of a muffin comes out clean. Let cool for about 15 minutes. Remove from the pan and let cool completely on a wire rack.

For Apple–Raisin Muffins

Substitute ½ cup golden raisins for the walnuts.

Per muffin: Calories 357, Protein 6 g, Fat 13 g, Carbohydrate 57 g, Fiber 8 g, Sodium 497 mg

Cranberry-Orange Muffins

☆☆☆☆☆☆☆☆☆☆☆☆☆☆☆☆☆☆☆☆☆☆☆

Makes 1 dozen muffins

These little gems are a treat. When you can't find fresh cranberries, frozen cranberries work perfectly. The sweetness of the orange balances the tartness of the cranberry, together creating a wonderful synergy of flavor. Organic cranberries are becoming increasingly available in many natural food stores so be sure to ask if you can't find them.

½ cup canola, safflower, or sunflower oil

½ cup maple syrup

Juice and zest of 2 oranges (about 1 cup juice, 4 tablespoons zest)

1 teaspoon apple cider vinegar

2 teaspoons vanilla

½ cup Sucanat, date sugar, or maple sugar

3½ cups barley flour

2 teaspoons baking soda

2 teaspoons baking powder

1 teaspoon ground cardamom

1 teaspoon salt

1½ cups chopped fresh or frozen cranberries (see Note)

2 teaspoons maple sugar, Sucanat, or date sugar

Preheat the oven to 350°F. Oil a 12-cup muffin pan or line it with unbleached paper liners and set aside.

Mix the oil, syrup, juice, zest, vinegar, and vanilla in a medium bowl.

In a separate, larger bowl, place the Sucanat; sift the flour, baking soda, baking powder, cardamom, and salt into the Sucanat. (Sifting isn't absolutely necessary, but it ensures there won't be clumps of flour or salt in the batter.) Whisk the wet ingredients into the dry ingredients. Do not overwork the batter. If the batter seems very stiff, add 1 or 2 tablespoons soymilk. Finish mixing with a spatula to scrape the sides of the bowl. Fold in the chopped cranberries.

Spoon the batter into the prepared pan. Sprinkle with the maple sugar.

Bake for 40 minutes and rotate the pan a half turn to ensure even baking. Bake 40 minutes more or until a knife inserted in the center of a muffin comes out clean. Let cool for about 10 minutes. Remove from the pan and let cool completely on a wire rack.

Note: If using frozen cranberries, do not thaw; to chop, pulse frozen berries in a food processor or blender. If using fresh cranberries, chop in a food processor or blender or by hand.

Per muffin: Calories 284, Protein 4 g, Fat 10 g, Carbohydrate 47 g, Fiber 6 g, Sodium 450 mg

Corn Muffins

☆ ☆

These are the first vegan corn muffins I've enjoyed in a long time. Older sister Karen was a corn muffin junky, addicted to Jiffy Mix. Hearts were crushed when we discovered lard in the list of ingredients. This recipe can be baked as bread (page 33) or as muffins.

½ cup canola, safflower, or sunflower oil

½ cup maple syrup

1¼ cups soymilk

2 teaspoons apple cider vinegar

2 teaspoons vanilla

½ cup Sucanat, date sugar, or maple sugar

1½ cups cornmeal*

3 cups barley flour

2 teaspoons baking soda

2 teaspoons baking powder

1 teaspoon salt

2 tablespoons maple sugar, Sucanat, or date sugar

*Note: You can substitute blue cornmeal for the yellow. It has a slightly nuttier flavor.

Preheat the oven to 350°F. Oil a 12-cup muffin pan or line it with unbleached paper liners, and set aside.

Mix the oil, syrup, soymilk, vinegar, and vanilla in a medium bowl.

In a separate, larger bowl, place the Sucanat and the cornmeal; sift the flour, baking soda, baking powder, cardamom, and salt into the cornmeal mixture. (Sifting isn't absolutely necessary, but it ensures there won't be clumps of flour or salt in the batter.) Whisk the wet ingredients into the dry ingredients. Do not overwork the batter. If the batter seems very stiff, add 1 to 2 tablespoons of soymilk. Finish mixing with a spatula to scrape the sides of the bowl.

Spoon the batter into the prepared pan. Sprinkle each muffin with maple sugar.

Bake for 20 minutes and rotate the pan a half turn to ensure even baking. Bake 5 to 6 minutes more or until a knife inserted in the center of a muffin comes out clean. Let cool for about 15 minutes. Remove from the pan and let cool completely on a wire rack.

For Blueberry Corn Muffins

Add 1½ cups blueberries to the batter.

For Orange Corn Muffins

Substitute the juice and zest of 2 oranges (about 1 cup juice and 5 to 6 tablespoons zest) for the soymilk.

 Per muffin: Calories 315, Protein 5 g, Fat 11 g, Carbohydrate 52 g, Fiber 6 g, Sodium 458 mg

Peach-Oat Bran Muffins

☆☆☆☆☆☆☆☆☆☆☆☆☆☆☆☆☆☆☆☆☆☆☆☆☆

Makes 1 dozen muffins

These muffins are perfectly sweet and delicious. Fresh, organic peaches usually show up in markets during the summer; until then they may be hard to find. When it is in-between the seasons, we recommend using frozen peaches.

Topping:

2 tablespoons maple sugar

1 tablespoon oat bran

¼ teaspoon ground cinnamon

Muffins:

½ cup canola, safflower, or sunflower oil

½ cup maple syrup

1¼ cups soymilk

2 teaspoons apple cider vinegar

2 teaspoons vanilla

¼ cup Sucanat, date sugar, or maple sugar

1 cup oat bran

3 cups barley flour

2 teaspoons baking soda

2 teaspoons baking powder

1 teaspoon ground cinnamon

Dash of grated nutmeg

1 teaspoon salt

2 peaches, pitted and chopped (about ¾ cup) (see Note)

Preheat the oven to 350°F. Oil a 12-cup muffin pan or line it with unbleached paper liners and set aside. In a small bowl, mix the topping ingredients; set aside.

Mix the oil, syrup, soymilk, vinegar, and vanilla in another small bowl.

In a separate, larger bowl, place the Sucanat and oat bran; sift the flour, baking soda, baking powder, cinnamon, nutmeg, and salt into the bran mixture. (Sifting isn't absolutely necessary, but it ensures there won't be clumps of flour or salt in the batter.) Whisk the wet ingredients into the dry ingredients. Do not overwork the batter. If the batter seems very stiff, add 1 tablespoon soymilk. Finish mixing with a spatula to scrape the sides of the bowl. Fold in the chopped peaches. Spoon the batter into the prepared pan. Sprinkle with the topping mixture.

Bake for 20 minutes and rotate the pan a half turn to ensure even baking. Bake 5 to 6 minutes more or until a knife inserted in the center of a muffin comes out clean. Let cool for about 15 minutes. Remove from the pan and let cool completely on a wire rack.

Note: If using frozen peaches, do not thaw; to chop, pulse frozen peaches in a food processor or blender. If using fresh peaches, chop by hand.

  Per muffin: Calories 278, Protein 6 g, Fat 11 g, Carbohydrate 45 g, Fiber 7 g, Sodium 454 mg

Mixed-Up Berry Muffins

☆ ☆

Makes 1 dozen muffins

Whether you use a frozen or fresh mix
of berries, these make wonderful
morning treats any time of the year.
The mix is totally up to you.

½ cup canola, safflower, or sunflower oil

½ cup maple syrup

1¼ cups soymilk

2 teaspoons apple cider vinegar

1 tablespoon vanilla

½ cup Sucanat, date sugar, or maple
   sugar

3½ cups barley flour

2 teaspoons baking soda

2 teaspoons baking powder

½ teaspoon ground cinnamon

Pinch of ground allspice

1 teaspoon salt

1½ cups mixture of whole frozen
   blueberries, raspberries, and
   blackberries

Topping:

¼ cup maple sugar, Sucanat,
   or date sugar

¼ cup whole berries

Preheat the oven to 350°F. Oil a 12-cup muffin pan or line it with unbleached paper liners and set aside.

Mix the oil, syrup, soymilk, vinegar, and vanilla in a small bowl.

In a separate, larger bowl, place the Sucanat; sift the flour, baking soda, baking powder, cinnamon, allspice, and salt into the Sucanat. (Sifting isn't absolutely necessary, but it ensures there won't be clumps of flour or salt in the batter.) Whisk the wet ingredients into the dry ingredients. Do not overwork the batter. If the batter seems very stiff, add 1 tablespoon soymilk. Finish mixing with a spatula to scrape the sides of the bowl. When the ingredients are well incorporated, fold in the berries.

Spoon the batter into the prepared pan. Sprinkle with maple sugar and place 3 or 4 whole berries on top of each muffin.

Bake for 25 minutes and rotate the pan a half turn to ensure even baking. Bake 5 to 6 minutes more or until a knife inserted in the center of a muffin comes out clean. Let cool for about 10 minutes. Remove from the pan and let cool completely on a wire rack.

Note: If using frozen berries, don't thaw before adding them to the batter or the batter will turn blue.

Per muffin: Calories 317, Protein 5 g, Fat 10 g,
Carbohydrate 54 g, Fiber 7 g, Sodium 455 mg

Cranberry-Orange Scones

Makes 8 scones

☆ ☆

The synergy of cranberry and orange is back in this delightful recipe. A wonderful combination with a cup of herbal tea.

⅓ cup canola, safflower, or sunflower oil

1 teaspoon apple cider vinegar

Juice and zest of 1 orange (½ cup juice, 2 tablespoons zest)

1 teaspoon vanilla

¼ cup plus 2 tablespoons Sucanat, date sugar, or maple sugar

2½ cups plus 2 tablespoons barley flour, divided

2 teaspoons baking soda

2 teaspoons baking powder

½ teaspoon ground cinnamon

½ teaspoon salt

¾ cup chopped fresh cranberries

Preheat the oven to 350°F. Oil a baking sheet and set aside.

Mix the oil, vinegar, juice, and vanilla in a small bowl.

In a separate, larger bowl, place the Sucanat; sift the 2½ cups flour, baking soda, baking powder, cinnamon, and salt into the Sucanat. (Sifting isn't absolutely necessary, but it ensures there won't be clumps of flour or salt in the batter.) Add the zest. Mix the wet ingredients into the dry with a spatula. Do not overwork the batter. The dough should be stiff but if it seems very stiff, add 1 or 2 tablespoons soymilk. Fold in the cranberries.

Knead the dough very lightly six or seven times (no more than 10) just until it forms a ball. Turn the ball of dough out onto a parchment-covered baking sheet. Dust with the remaining 2 tablespoons flour and pat the dough into a dome shape about 2 inches thick. With a large knife, score the dough into 8 even wedges.

Bake for 20 minutes, rotate the pan a half turn to ensure even baking, and bake 5 to 6 minutes more or until a knife inserted in the center of a scone comes out clean. Let cool for 15 to 20 minutes. Remove from the pan and let cool completely on a wire rack 15 minutes before slicing.

  Per scone: Calories 255, Protein 5 g, Fat 9 g, Carbohydrate 41 g, Fiber 7 g, Sodium 540 mg

Raisin-Pecan Scones

Makes 8 scones

☆ ☆

These are a sweet, nutty, morning treat. Currants may be used instead of the raisins; they are slightly smaller and not quite as sweet.

⅓ cup canola, safflower, or sunflower oil

2 tablespoons maple syrup

½ cup soymilk

1 teaspoon apple cider vinegar

1 teaspoon vanilla

¼ cup Sucanat, date sugar, or maple sugar

2½ cups plus 2 tablespoons barley flour, divided

2 teaspoons baking soda

2 teaspoons baking powder

½ teaspoon ground cinnamon

½ teaspoon salt

1 cup raisins

¾ cup chopped pecans

Preheat the oven to 350°F. Oil a baking sheet and set aside.

Mix the oil, syrup, soymilk, vinegar, and vanilla in a small bowl.

In a separate, larger bowl, place the Sucanat; sift the 2½ cups flour, baking soda, baking powder, cinnamon, and salt into the Sucanat. (Sifting isn't absolutely necessary, but it ensures there won't be clumps of flour or salt in the batter.) Mix the wet ingredients into the dry with a spatula. Do not overwork the batter. The dough should be stiff but if it seems very stiff, add 1 or 2 tablespoons soymilk. Work in the raisins and the pecans.

Knead the dough very lightly six or seven times (no more than 10) just until it forms a ball. Turn the ball of dough out onto a parchment-covered baking sheet. Dust with the remaining 2 tablespoons flour and pat the dough into a dome shape about 2 inches thick. With a large knife, score the dough into 8 even wedges.

Bake for 20 minutes, rotate the pan a half turn to ensure even baking, and bake 5 to 6 minutes more or until a knife inserted in the center of a scone comes out clean. Let cool for 15 to 20 minutes. Remove from the pan and let cool completely on a wire rack 15 minutes before slicing.

Per scone: Calories 375, Protein 6 g, Fat 17 g, Carbohydrate 55 g, Fiber 9 g, Sodium 547 mg

Chocolate Chip Scones

☆ ☆

Makes 8 scones

This is another version of the traditional scone. We've added chocolate chips to bring a bit more appeal to this classic biscuit. It is the perfect breakfast treat, not too sweet. Vegan carob chips can always be used in place of the chocolate for a caffeine-free alternative.

⅓ cup canola, safflower, or sunflower oil

2 tablespoons maple syrup

½ cup soymilk

1 teaspoon apple cider vinegar

1 teaspoon vanilla

¼ cup Sucanat, date sugar, or maple sugar

2½ cups plus 2 tablespoons barley flour, divided

2 teaspoons baking soda

2 teaspoons baking powder

½ teaspoon ground cinnamon

½ teaspoon salt

¼ teaspoon grated nutmeg

¾ cup chocolate chips

Preheat the oven to 350°F. Oil a baking sheet and set aside.

Mix the oil, syrup, soymilk, vinegar, and vanilla in a small bowl.

In a separate, larger bowl, place the Sucanat; sift the 2½ cups flour, baking soda, baking powder, cinnamon, salt, and nutmeg into the Sucanat. (Sifting isn't absolutely necessary, but it ensures there won't be clumps of flour or salt in the batter.) Mix the wet ingredients into the dry with a spatula. Do not overwork the batter. The dough should be stiff, but if it seems very stiff, add 1 or 2 tablespoons soymilk. Work in the chocolate chips.

Knead the dough very lightly six or seven times (no more than 10) just until it forms a ball. Turn the ball of dough out onto a parchment-covered baking sheet. Dust with the remaining 2 tablespoons flour and pat the dough into a dome shape about 2 inches thick. With a large knife, score the dough into 8 even wedges.

Bake for 20 minutes, rotate the pan a half turn to ensure even baking, and bake 5 to 6 minutes more or until a knife inserted in the center of a scone comes out clean. Let cool for 15 to 20 minutes. Remove from the pan and let cool completely on a wire rack 15 minutes before slicing.

For Blueberry Scones

Omit chocolate chips. Add ¾ cup blueberries.

Per scone: Calories 333, Protein 6 g, Fat 14 g, Carbohydrate 48 g, Fiber 7 g, Sodium 542 mg

Banana Nut Bread

☆ ☆

Makes one 8 x 4 x 2½" loaf
(12 servings)

This hearty bread takes care of those overripe bananas sitting in the pantry! I love this recipe. The walnuts are amazing in this bread and I highly recommend using them.

2 or 3 very ripe bananas (for 1 cup mashed)

¼ cup canola, safflower, or sunflower oil

¼ cup maple syrup

1 cup soymilk

1 teaspoon apple cider vinegar

2 teaspoons vanilla

¼ cup Sucanat, date sugar, or maple sugar

¾ cup chopped walnuts

1¾ cups barley flour

1 teaspoon baking soda

1 teaspoon baking powder

½ teaspoon ground cinnamon

½ teaspoon salt

Topping:

3 tablespoons walnut halves

1 tablespoon maple sugar, Sucanat, or date sugar

Preheat the oven to 350°F. Oil an 8 x 4 x 2½" loaf pan and set aside.

In a small bowl, mash the bananas, leaving some pieces big enough to be recognized as a banana chunk. If the bananas are very ripe, chop them with a knife instead of mashing.

Mix the mashed bananas, oil, syrup, soymilk, vinegar, and vanilla in another small bowl.

In a separate, larger bowl, mix the Sucanat and walnuts; sift the flour, baking soda, baking powder, cinnamon, and salt into the walnut mixture. (Sifting isn't absolutely necessary, but it ensures there won't be clumps of flour or salt in the batter.) Whisk the wet ingredients into the dry ingredients. Do not overwork the batter. If the batter seems very stiff, add 1 tablespoon soymilk. Finish mixing with a spatula to scrape the sides of the bowl. Mix just until the ingredients are well incorporated.

Pour the batter into the prepared pan. Top the loaf with walnut halves and sprinkle with maple sugar.

Bake for 40 minutes. Rotate the pan a half turn to ensure even baking, and bake 40 to 45 minutes more or until a knife inserted in the center comes out clean. Let cool for 15 to 20 minutes. Remove from the pan and let cool completely on a wire rack before slicing.

For a low-fat, low-sugar Banana Bread

Omit the walnuts and topping, and reduce the Sucanat and oil by half, to 2 tablespoons each.

Per serving: Calories 205, Protein 4 g, Fat 11 g, Carbohydrate 25 g, Fiber 3 g, Sodium 228 mg

Banana Carob Chip Bread

☆ **Makes one 8 x 4 x 2½" loaf (12 servings)**

This is a favorite at the Orleans Whole Food store in Orleans, Massachusetts. The idea of combining carob chips and banana was brought about by Richard, a thoughtful and faithful Simple Treats supporter.

2 or 3 very ripe bananas (for 1 cup mashed)

¾ cup carob chips

¼ cup canola, safflower, or sunflower oil

¼ cup maple syrup

¾ cup soymilk

1 teaspoon apple cider vinegar

2 teaspoons vanilla

¼ cup Sucanat, date sugar, or maple sugar

¾ cup chopped walnuts

1¾ cups barley flour

1 teaspoon baking soda

1 teaspoon baking powder

½ teaspoon ground cinnamon

½ teaspoon salt

Preheat the oven to 350°F. Oil an 8 x 4 x 2½" loaf pan and set aside.

In a small bowl, mash the bananas, leaving some pieces big enough to be recognized as a banana chunk. If the bananas are very ripe, chop them with a knife instead of mashing.

Mix the mashed bananas, carob chips, oil, syrup, soymilk, vinegar, and vanilla in another small bowl.

In a separate, larger bowl, mix the Sucanat and walnuts; sift the flour, baking soda, baking powder, cinnamon, and salt into the walnut mixture. (Sifting isn't absolutely necessary, but it ensures there won't be clumps of flour or salt in the batter.) Whisk the wet ingredients into the dry ingredients. Do not overwork the batter. If the batter seems very stiff, add 1 tablespoon soymilk. Finish mixing with a spatula to scrape the sides of the bowl. Mix just until the ingredients are well incorporated.

Pour the batter into the prepared pan. Bake for 40 minutes. Rotate the pan a half turn to ensure even baking, and bake 40 to 45 minutes more or until a knife inserted in the center comes out clean. Let cool for 15 to 20 minutes. Remove from the pan and let cool completely on a wire rack before slicing.

For a nutty sweet addition, top the loaf with walnut halves and sprinkle with maple sugar.

Per serving: Calories 234, Protein 4 g, Fat 11 g, Carbohydrate 31 g, Fiber 4 g, Sodium 229 mg

Carrot Nut Bread

☆ ☆

**Makes one 8 x 4 x 2½" loaf
(12 servings)**

This is a wholesome, veganized version of an old favorite. It is perfectly moist and wonderfully sweet. It also makes the house smell incredibly aromatic.

¼ cup canola, safflower, or sunflower oil

¼ cup maple syrup

2 tablespoons barley malt syrup

1 cup soymilk

1 teaspoon apple cider vinegar

1 teaspoon vanilla

½ cup chopped walnuts (optional)

2 tablespoons Sucanat, date sugar, or maple sugar

1¾ cups barley flour

1 teaspoon baking soda

1 teaspoon baking powder

½ tablespoon salt

1 teaspoon ground cinnamon

½ tablespoon powdered ginger

½ tablespoon ground cloves

½ tablespoon ground allspice

¼ teaspoon grated nutmeg

2¼ cups shredded carrots, loosely packed

½ cup raisins (optional)

Topping:

¼ cup chopped walnuts

Preheat the oven to 350°F. Oil an 8 x 4 x 2½" loaf pan and set aside.

Mix the oil, syrups, soymilk, vinegar, and vanilla in a small bowl.

In a separate, larger bowl, place the chopped walnuts, if using, and Sucanat; sift the flour, baking soda, baking powder, spices, and salt into the walnut mixture. (Sifting isn't absolutely necessary, but it ensures there won't be clumps of flour or salt in the batter.) Whisk the wet ingredients into the dry ingredients. Do not overwork the batter. If the batter seems very stiff, add 1 tablespoon soymilk. Finish mixing with a spatula to scrape the sides of the bowl. Fold in the carrots and raisins, if using.

Pour the batter into the prepared pan. Sprinkle with ¼ cup chopped walnuts.

Bake for 40 minutes, rotate the pan a half turn to ensure even baking, and bake 35 to 40 minutes more or until a knife inserted in the center comes out clean. Let cool for 15 to 20 minutes. Remove from pan and let cool completely on a wire rack.

For Low-Fat Carrot Bread

Omit the walnuts. Use 2 tablespoons canola, safflower, or sunflower oil; 1 tablespoon barley malt syrup; ¾ cup soymilk; and 1 tablespoon Sucanat.

Per serving: Calories 168, Protein 3 g, Fat 7 g, Carbohydrate 25 g, Fiber 4 g, Sodium 235 mg

Cornbread

☆ *Makes one 9" square or round (12 servings)*

This is a variation on our whole-grain corn muffins. More of a savory version, it goes really well with spreads and dips. It is also a fantastic accompaniment to a bowl of vegan chili.

½ cup canola, safflower, or sunflower oil

¼ cup maple syrup

1¼ cups soymilk

2 tablespoons apple cider vinegar

¼ cup Sucanat, date sugar, or maple sugar

1½ cups cornmeal

2¾ cups barley flour

2 tablespoons baking soda

2 tablespoons baking powder

½ teaspoon paprika

⅛ teaspoon cayenne pepper

⅛ teaspoon chili powder

⅛ teaspoon cumin

1 teaspoon salt

½ cup fresh or frozen corn kernels (optional)

Topping:

¼ teaspoon paprika

2 tablespoons Sucanat, date sugar, or maple sugar

Preheat the oven to 350°F. Oil a 9" square or round cake pan and set aside.

Mix the oil, syrup, soymilk, and vinegar in a small bowl.

In a separate, larger bowl, place the Sucanat and the cornmeal; sift the flour, the baking soda, baking powder, spices, and salt into the cornmeal mixture. (Sifting isn't absolutely necessary, but it ensures there won't be clumps of flour or salt in the batter.) Whisk the wet ingredients into the dry ingredients. Do not overwork the batter. If the batter seems very stiff, add 1 tablespoon soymilk. Finish mixing with a spatula to scrape the sides of the bowl. Fold in the corn.

Pour the batter into the prepared pan. Sprinkle with the paprika and Sucanat. Bake for 25 minutes, rotate the pan a half turn to ensure even baking, and bake 5 to 6 minutes more or until a knife inserted in the center comes out clean. Let cool for 15 minutes. Remove from the pan and let cool completely on a wire rack.

For Spicy Cornbread

Add 1 to 2 tablespoons minced jalapeño pepper.

 Per serving: Calories 284, Protein 5 g, Fat 11 g, Carbohydrate 44 g, Fiber 6 g, Sodium 999 mg

Lemon Poppy Tea Bread

☆ ☆

**Makes one 8 x 4 x 2½" loaf
(12 servings)**

*This bread is light and satisfying with a
refreshing kick of lemon.*

Topping:

¾ teaspoon poppy seeds

2 teaspoons maple sugar

Bread:

¼ cup canola, safflower, or sunflower oil

¼ cup maple syrup

½ cup soymilk

Juice and zest of 1 lemon (about ¼ cup
juice, 1 tablespoon zest)

1 teaspoon vanilla

2 teaspoons lemon extract

1 tablespoon poppy seeds

¼ cup Sucanat, date sugar, or maple
sugar

2 cups barley flour

1 teaspoon baking soda

1 teaspoon baking powder

½ teaspoon salt

Preheat the oven to 350°F. Oil an 8 x 4 x 2½" loaf pan and set aside. In a small bowl, mix the topping ingredients; set aside.

Mix the oil, syrup, soymilk, juice, zest, vanilla, and lemon extract in another small bowl.

In a separate, larger bowl, place 1 tablespoon of the poppy seeds and the Sucanat; sift the flour, baking soda, baking powder, and salt into the poppy seed mixture. (Sifting isn't absolutely necessary, but it ensures there won't be clumps of flour or salt in the batter.) Whisk the wet ingredients into the dry ingredients. Do not overwork the batter. If the batter seems very stiff, add 1 to 2 tablespoons soymilk. Finish mixing with a spatula to scrape the sides of the bowl.

Pour the batter into the prepared pan. Sprinkle with the topping mixture.

Bake for 30 minutes, rotate the pan a half turn to ensure even baking, and bake 20 to 25 minutes more or until a knife inserted in the center comes out clean. Let cool for 15 minutes. Remove from the pan and let cool completely on a wire rack.

Per serving: Calories 152, Protein 3 g, Fat 6 g,
Carbohydrate 24 g, Fiber 4 g, Sodium 227 mg

Chocolate Chip Loaf

☆ ☆ ☆ ☆ ☆ ☆ ☆ ☆ ☆ ☆ ☆ ☆ ☆ ☆ ☆ ☆ ☆ ☆ ☆ ☆

This breakfast treat was inspired by Sunday morning trips to Eagerman's bakery in Natick, Massachusetts. We would pick up a dozen bagels and just maybe, an Entenmann's chocolate chip loaf. This recipe comes pretty close to the other version; I love this bread with a cup of peppermint tea.

Topping:

3 tablespoons roughly chopped chocolate chips

1½ teaspoons maple sugar

Loaf:

¼ cup canola, safflower, or sunflower oil

¼ cup maple syrup

¾ cup soymilk

1 teaspoon apple cider vinegar

2 teaspoons vanilla

¼ cup Sucanat, date sugar, or maple sugar

1¾ cups barley flour

1 teaspoon baking soda

1 teaspoon baking powder

¼ teaspoon grated nutmeg

½ teaspoon salt

¾ cup roughly chopped chocolate chips

Preheat the oven to 350°F. Oil an 8 x 4 x 2½" loaf pan and set aside. In a small bowl, mix the chopped chocolate chips and maple sugar; set aside.

Mix the oil, syrup, soymilk, vinegar, and vanilla in another small bowl.

In a separate, larger bowl, place the Sucanat; sift the flour, baking soda, baking powder, nutmeg, and salt into the chocolate chip mixture. (Sifting isn't absolutely necessary, but it ensures there won't be clumps of flour or salt in the batter.) Whisk the wet ingredients into the dry ingredients. Do not overwork the batter. If the batter seems very stiff, add 1 tablespoon soymilk. Fold in ¾ cup chopped chocolate chips.

Pour the batter into the prepared pan. Sprinkle with the topping mixture.

Bake for 40 minutes, rotate the pan a half turn to ensure even baking, and bake 35 to 40 minutes more or until a knife inserted in the center of a muffin comes out clean. Let cool for 15 minutes. Remove from the pan and let cool completely on a wire rack.

For Raspberry Chocolate Chip Loaf

Reduce chocolate chips to ½ cup; increase the soymilk to 1 cup; add ½ cup fresh or frozen raspberries, ⅛ teaspoon nutmeg, and 1 teaspoon raspberry extract.

Per serving: Calories 209, Protein 3 g, Fat 9 g, Carbohydrate 30 g, Fiber 3 g, Sodium 227 mg

Pumpkin Spice Bread

☆ ☆

Makes one 8 x 4 x 2½" loaf
(12 servings)

This bread is filled with the warming spices of autumn and is ideal when fresh pumpkin is available. If it's too much trouble to deal with the whole pumpkin, or you are unable to find it, organic canned pumpkin is available in most natural food stores.

Topping:

2 teaspoons maple sugar, Sucanat, or date sugar

2 teaspoons barley flour

1 teaspoon ground cinnamon

Bread:

¾ cup pumpkin purée

¼ cup canola, safflower, or sunflower oil

¼ cup maple syrup

¾ cup soymilk

1 teaspoon apple cider vinegar

2 teaspoons vanilla

¼ cup Sucanat, date sugar, or maple sugar

1¾ cup barley flour

1 teaspoon baking soda

1 teaspoon baking powder

2 teaspoons ground cinnamon

1 teaspoon powdered ginger

½ teaspoon ground allspice

¼ teaspoon ground cloves

Dash of grated nutmeg

½ teaspoon salt

Preheat the oven to 350°F. Oil an an 8 x 4 x 2½" loaf pan and set aside. In a small bowl, mix topping ingredients; set aside.

Mix the pumpkin, oil, syrup, soymilk, vinegar, and vanilla in another small bowl.

In a separate, larger bowl, place the Sucanat; sift the flour, baking soda, baking powder, spices, and salt into the Sucanat. (Sifting isn't absolutely necessary, but it ensures there won't be clumps of flour or salt in the batter.) Whisk the wet ingredients into the dry ingredients. Do not overwork the batter. If the batter seems very stiff, add 1 teaspoon soymilk. Finish mixing with a spatula to scrape the sides of the bowl. Mix just until ingredients are well incorporated.

Pour the batter into the prepared pan. Sprinkle with the topping mixture.

Bake for 40 minutes, rotate the pan a half turn to ensure even baking, and bake 40 minutes more or until a knife inserted in the center comes out clean. Let cool for 15 to 20 minutes. Remove from the pan and let cool completely on a wire rack.

Per serving: Calories 145, Protein 3 g, Fat 5 g, Carbohydrate 23 g, Fiber 4 g, Sodium 227 mg

Ginger-Pear Spice Loaf

☆ ☆

Makes one 8 x 4 x 2½" loaf
(12 servings)

This cake is filled with the intoxicating essence of ginger, accompanied in this recipe by the perfectly sweet flavor of pears—an energizing and satisfying treat.

Topping:

1 teaspoon barley flour

2 teaspoons maple sugar, Sucanat, or date sugar

1 teaspoon ground cinnamon

Pinch of salt

Loaf:

¼ cup canola, safflower, or sunflower oil

¼ cup maple syrup

¾ cup soymilk

1 teaspoon apple cider vinegar

1 teaspoon vanilla

¼ cup plus 1 teaspoon Sucanat, date sugar, or maple sugar

1¾ cups barley flour

1 teaspoon baking soda

1 teaspoon baking powder

2 teaspoons powdered ginger

1½ teaspoons ground cinnamon

¼ teaspoon ground allspice

¼ teaspoon grated nutmeg

¼ teaspoon ground cloves

½ teaspoon salt

1 medium or 2 small pears, cored and chopped

Preheat the oven to 350°F. Oil an 8 x 4 x 2½" loaf pan and set aside. In a small bowl, mix topping ingredients; set aside.

Mix the oil, syrup, soymilk, vinegar, and vanilla in another small bowl.

In a separate, larger bowl, place the Sucanat; sift the flour, baking soda, baking powder, spices, and salt into the Sucanat. (Sifting isn't absolutely necessary, but it ensures there won't be clumps of flour or salt in the batter.) Whisk the wet ingredients into the dry ingredients. Do not overwork the batter. If the batter seems very stiff, add 1 tablespoon soymilk. Finish mixing with a spatula to scrape the sides of the bowl. When all the ingredients are well incorporated, fold in the chopped pears.

Pour the batter into the prepared pan. Sprinkle with the topping mixture.

Bake for 45 minutes, rotate the pan a half turn to ensure even baking, and bake 40 minutes more or until a knife inserted in the center comes out clean. Let cool for 10 minutes. Remove from the pan and let cool completely on a wire rack.

Per serving: Calories 159, Protein 3 g, Fat 5 g,
Carbohydrate 27 g, Fiber 4 g, Sodium 227 mg

Gingerbread

☆ **Makes one 8 x 4 x 2½" loaf (12 servings)**

This recipe was created during the winter, for a bread filled with raisins, spices, and the glorious taste of ginger. We use organic blackstrap molasses to give a deep dark color and full-bodied taste. Molasses is an energy-building food, making it perfect for those extra-cold winter days, when all of the senses need some warming!

Topping:

2 teaspoons maple sugar, Sucanat, or date sugar

2 teaspoons barley flour

1 teaspoon ground cinnamon

Bread:

¼ cup canola, safflower, or sunflower oil

¼ cup maple syrup

3 tablespoons molasses

¾ cup soymilk

1 teaspoon apple cider vinegar

2 teaspoons vanilla

½ cup raisins

¼ cup Sucanat, date sugar, or maple sugar

1¾ cups barley flour

1 teaspoon baking soda

1 teaspoon baking powder

2 teaspoons powdered ginger

2 teaspoons ground cinnamon

½ teaspoon ground allspice

½ teaspoon salt

Preheat the oven to 350°F. Oil an 8 x 4 x 2½" loaf pan and set aside. In a small bowl, mix the topping ingredients; set aside.

Mix the oil, syrup, molasses, soymilk, vinegar, and vanilla in another small bowl.

In a separate, larger bowl, place the raisins and the Sucanat; sift the flour, baking soda, baking powder, spices, and salt into the raisin mixture. (Sifting isn't absolutely necessary, but it ensures there won't be clumps of flour or salt in the batter.) Whisk the wet ingredients into the dry ingredients. Do not overwork the batter. If the batter seems very stiff, add 1 to 2 tablespoons soymilk. Finish mixing with a spatula to scrape the sides of the bowl.

Pour the batter into the prepared pan. Sprinkle with the topping mixture.

Bake for 40 minutes, rotate the pan a half turn to ensure even baking, and bake 30 to 35 minutes more or until a knife inserted in the center comes out clean. Let cool for 15 minutes. Remove from the pan and let cool completely on a wire rack.

Tip: Lightly coat the tablespoon measure with oil before measuring the molasses; the molasses will slide right off the spoon for easy cleanup.

★ Per serving: Calories 172, Protein 3 g, Fat 5 g, Carbohydrate 30 g, Fiber 4 g, Sodium 231 mg ★

Fig-Walnut Bread

☆ ☆

**Makes one 8 x 4 x 2½" loaf
(12 servings)**

I love this bread. It has such a lovely sweet flavor. The walnuts, figs, and hint of cinnamon are a really nice combination.

¼ cup canola, safflower, or sunflower oil

¼ cup maple syrup

1 cup soymilk

1 teaspoon apple cider vinegar

2 teaspoons vanilla

½ cup chopped walnuts

¼ cup Sucanat, date sugar, or maple sugar

1¾ cups barley flour

1 teaspoon baking soda

1 teaspoon baking powder

1 teaspoon ground cinnamon

½ teaspoon salt

1 cup chopped, dried figs (see Note)

Topping:

2 tablespoons chopped walnuts

Preheat the oven to 350°F. Oil an 8 x 4 x 2½" loaf pan and set aside.

Mix oil, syrup, soymilk, vinegar, and vanilla in a small bowl.

In a separate, larger bowl, place ½ cup walnuts and the Sucanat; sift the flour, baking soda, baking powder, cinnamon, and salt into the Sucanat. (Sifting isn't absolutely necessary, but it ensures there won't be clumps of flour or salt in the batter.) Whisk the wet ingredients into the dry ingredients. Do not overwork the batter. If the batter seems very stiff, add 1 tablespoon soymilk. Finish mixing with a spatula to scrape the sides of the bowl. Fold in the figs.

Pour the batter into the prepared pan. Sprinkle with 2 tablespoons walnuts.

Bake for 35 minutes, rotate the pan a half turn to ensure even baking, and bake 35 minutes more or until a knife inserted in the center comes out clean. Let cool for 15 minutes before slicing.

Note: If you use a food processor or blender to chop figs, add ½ cup of the barley flour to the figs and pulse on and off to keep figs from clumping. Do not let the machine run continuously.

Per serving: Calories 223, Protein 4 g, Fat 9 g, Carbohydrate 34 g, Fiber 5 g, Sodium 230 mg

Raspberry Lime Bread

☆ ☆

**Makes one 8 x 4 x 2½" loaf
(12 servings)**

One day, while reminiscing about the taste of Raspberry Lime Rickeys, I thought, "What a great flavor for a bread!" This recipe was created in hopes of capturing the spark of these two flavors and bringing them together for something completely special.

Topping:

- 1 tablespoon maple sugar, Sucanat, or date sugar
- 2 teaspoons barley flour

Bread:

- ¼ cup canola, safflower, or sunflower oil
- ¼ cup maple syrup
- ¾ cup soymilk
- Juice and zest of 1 lime (about 2 tablespoons juice, 1 tablespoon zest)
- ¼ teaspoon apple cider vinegar
- 1 teaspoon raspberry extract
- 1 teaspoon vanilla
- ¼ cup Sucanat, date sugar, or maple sugar
- 1¾ cup barley flour
- 1 teaspoon baking soda
- 1 teaspoon baking powder
- ¼ teaspoon ground cinnamon
- ⅛ teaspoon ground cloves
- ½ teaspoon salt
- ¾ cup chopped raspberries

Preheat the oven to 350°F. Oil an 8 x 4 x 2½" loaf pan and set aside. In a small bowl, mix the topping ingredients; set aside.

Mix oil, syrup, soymilk, juice, zest, vinegar, raspberry extract, and vanilla in another small bowl.

In a separate, larger bowl, place the Sucanat; sift the flour, baking soda, baking powder, cinnamon, cloves, and salt into the Sucanat. (Sifting isn't absolutely necessary, but it ensures there won't be clumps of flour or salt in the batter.) Whisk the wet ingredients into the dry ingredients. Do not overwork the batter. If the batter seems very stiff, add 1 tablespoon soymilk. Finish mixing with a spatula to scrape the sides of the bowl. Fold in the raspberries.

Pour the batter into the prepared pan. Sprinkle with the topping mixture.

Bake for 40 minutes, rotate the pan a half turn to ensure even baking, and bake 40 minutes more or until a knife inserted in the center comes out clean. Let cool for 15 minutes before slicing.

Note: If using frozen raspberries, do not thaw; to chop, pulse frozen berries in a food processor or blender. If using fresh raspberries, chop in a food processor or blender or by hand.

Per serving: Calories 148, Protein 3 g, Fat 5 g, Carbohydrate 24 g, Fiber 4 g, Sodium 227 mg

Sweet Potato-Pecan Bread

☆ ☆

Makes one 8 x 4 x 2½" loaf
(12 servings)

Filled with beta-carotene, sweet potatoes are just too delicious to keep exclusively for our brownie recipe. Here they star in this wonderfully warming, spice-filled bread.

Topping:

2 teaspoons maple sugar, Sucanat, or date sugar

2 teaspoons barley flour

1 teaspoon ground cinnamon

3 tablespoons whole pecans

Bread:

¾ cup Sweet Potato Purée (next column)

¼ cup canola, safflower, or sunflower oil

¼ cup maple syrup

¾ cup soymilk

1 teaspoon apple cider vinegar

2 teaspoons vanilla

¼ cup Sucanat, date sugar, or maple sugar

½ cup coarsely chopped pecans or walnuts

1¾ cups barley flour

1 teaspoon baking soda

1 teaspoon baking powder

2 teaspoons ground cinnamon

½ teaspoon ground allspice

Dash of grated nutmeg

½ teaspoon salt

Preheat the oven to 350°F. Oil an 8 x 4 x 2½" loaf pan and set aside. In a small bowl, mix the topping ingredients; set aside.

Mix Sweet Potato Purée, oil, syrup, soymilk, vinegar, and vanilla in a medium bowl.

In a separate, larger bowl, place the Sucanat and nuts. Sift the flour, baking soda, baking powder, spices, and salt into the Sucanat. (Sifting isn't absolutely necessary, but it ensures there won't be clumps of flour or salt in the batter.) Whisk the wet ingredients into the dry ingredients. Do not overwork the batter. If the batter seems very stiff, add 1 teaspoon soymilk. Finish mixing with a spatula to scrape the sides of the bowl. Mix just until all of the ingredients are incorporated.

Pour the batter into the prepared pan. Sprinkle with the topping mixture.

Bake for 35 minutes, rotate the pan a half turn to ensure even baking, and bake 35 minutes more or until a knife inserted in the center comes out clean. Let cool for 15 minutes before slicing.

For Sweet Potato Purée

Peel and cut 1 sweet potato into chunks; steam or boil 10 to 15 minutes or until tender. Or, use organic, canned sweet potatoes. When the sweet potato is tender, drain, reserving some of the cooking liquid. Purée in a food processor or blender, adding the reserved cooking liquid a little at a time to thin the purée if necessary. The purée should be slightly thinner than mashed potatoes.

Per serving: Calories 202, Protein 3 g, Fat 10 g, Carbohydrate 28 g, Fiber 4 g, Sodium 228 mg

Zucchini Bread

☆ ☆ ☆ ☆ ☆ ☆ ☆ ☆ ☆ ☆ ☆ ☆ ☆ ☆ ☆ ☆ ☆ ☆ ☆ ☆

**Makes one 8 x 4 x 2½" loaf
(12 servings)**

By the end of summer everyone is wondering what to do with all of the squash coming up in the garden! Here's the answer. This bread is perfectly moist and wonderfully sweet. The nuts offer wonderful texture and flavor, but can always be omitted.

¼ cup canola, safflower, or sunflower oil

¼ cup maple syrup

1 cup soymilk

1 teaspoon apple cider vinegar

1 teaspoon vanilla

½ cup chopped walnuts (optional)

¼ cup Sucanat, date sugar, or maple sugar

1¾ cups barley flour

1 teaspoon baking soda

1 teaspoon baking powder

2 teaspoons ground cinnamon

½ teaspoon ground allspice

¼ teaspoon grated nutmeg

½ teaspoon salt

1¼ cups shredded zucchini (1 medium to large) or summer squash, lightly packed

½ cup raisins (optional)

Topping:

¼ cup chopped walnuts (optional)

Preheat the oven to 350°F. Oil an 8 x 4 x 2½" loaf pan and set aside.

Mix the oil, syrup, soymilk, vinegar, and vanilla in a small bowl.

In a separate, larger bowl, place ½ cup walnuts, if using, and the Sucanat; sift the flour, baking soda, baking powder, spices, and salt into the walnut mixture. (Sifting isn't absolutely necessary, but it ensures there won't be clumps of flour or salt in the batter.) Whisk the wet ingredients into the dry ingredients. Do not overwork the batter. If the batter seems very stiff, add 1 tablespoon soymilk. Finish mixing with a spatula to scrape the sides of the bowl. When all of the ingredients are well incorporated, fold in the zucchini and raisins, if using.

Pour the batter into the prepared pan. Sprinkle with ¼ cup chopped walnuts if desired.

Bake for 40 minutes, rotate the pan a half turn to ensure even baking, and bake 40 minutes more or until a knife inserted in the center comes out clean. Let cool for 15 minutes before slicing.

Per serving: Calories 142, Protein 3 g, Fat 5 g, Carbohydrate 22 g, Fiber 3 g, Sodium 228 mg

Cranberry Walnut Bread

☆☆☆☆☆☆☆☆☆☆☆☆☆☆☆☆☆☆☆☆☆☆

**Makes one 8 x 4 x 2½" loaf
(12 servings)**

This bread is always a favorite, especially here on Cape Cod where there is an abundance of fresh local cranberries. Actually a shrub, they are mainly grown here in New England in wet, boggy areas. If you can't find fresh cranberries, frozen work equally well.

Topping:

¼ cup fresh or frozen cranberries, chopped

1 tablespoon maple sugar, Sucanat, or date sugar

1 teaspoon barley flour

Bread:

¼ cup canola, sunflower, or safflower oil

¼ cup maple syrup

1 cup soymilk

1 teaspoon apple cider vinegar

1 teaspoon vanilla

¼ cup Sucanat, date sugar, or maple sugar

1¾ cups barley flour

1 teaspoon baking soda

1 teaspoon baking powder

½ teaspoon ground cinnamon

½ teaspoon salt

¾ cup chopped walnuts

¾ cup fresh or frozen cranberries, chopped (see Note)

Preheat the oven to 350°F. Oil an 8 x 4 x 2½" loaf pan and set aside. In a small bowl, mix the topping ingredients; set aside.

Mix the oil, syrup, soymilk, vinegar, and vanilla in another small bowl.

In a separate, larger bowl, place the Sucanat; sift the flour, baking soda, baking powder, cinnamon, and salt into the Sucanat. (Sifting isn't absolutely necessary, but it ensures there won't be clumps of flour or salt in the batter.) Whisk the wet ingredients into the dry ingredients. Do not overwork the batter. If the batter seems very stiff, add 1 tablespoon soymilk. Finish mixing with a spatula to scrape the sides of the bowl. When all of the ingredients are well incorporated, fold in the walnuts and ¾ cup cranberries.

Pour the batter into the prepared pan. Sprinkle with the topping mixture.

Bake for 40 minutes, rotate the pan a half turn to ensure even baking, and bake 40 minutes more or until a knife inserted in the center of a muffin comes out clean. Let cool for 10 minutes before slicing.

Note: If using frozen cranberries, do not thaw; to chop, pulse frozen berries in a food processor or blender. If using fresh cranberries, chop in a food processor or blender or by hand.

Per serving: Calories 195, Protein 4 g, Fat 10 g, Carbohydrate 25 g, Fiber 4 g, Sodium 228 mg

Date Nut Bread

☆ ☆

Makes one 8 x 4 x 2½" loaf
(12 servings)

This bread is so moist and tender. The dried dates confer a lovely, natural sweetness to this recipe. My mother loves date nut bread with cream cheese —we are still working on the vegan cream cheese part.

1¾ cups dried, pitted dates

¼ cup canola oil

¼ cup maple syrup

1 cup soymilk

1 teaspoon apple cider vinegar

2 teaspoons vanilla

½ cup chopped walnuts

2 tablespoons Sucanat, date sugar, or maple sugar

1¾ cups barley flour

1 teaspoon baking soda

1 teaspoon baking powder

½ teaspoon ground cinnamon

½ teaspoon salt

Topping:

2 tablespoons chopped walnuts

Preheat the oven to 350°F. Oil an 8 x 4 x 2½" loaf pan and set aside.

Chop dates by hand or in a food processor or blender. If you're using a food processor or blender, add ½ cup of the flour to the machine with the dates to keep them from clumping, and pulse on and off. Do not run the machine continuously. Set aside.

Mix the oil, syrup, soymilk, vinegar, and vanilla in a small bowl.

In a separate, larger bowl, place the ½ cup walnuts and Sucanat; sift the flour, baking soda, baking powder, cinnamon, and salt into the walnut mixture. (Sifting isn't absolutely necessary, but it ensures there won't be clumps of flour or salt in the batter.) Whisk the wet ingredients into the dry ingredients. Do not overwork the batter. If the batter seems very stiff, add 1 tablespoon soymilk. Finish mixing with a spatula to scrape the sides of the bowl. When all of the ingredients are well incorporated, fold in the chopped dates.

Pour the batter into the prepared pan. Sprinkle with the 2 tablespoons walnuts.

Bake for 35 minutes, rotate the pan a half turn to ensure even baking, and bake 35 minutes more or until a knife inserted in the center comes out clean. Let cool for 15 minutes before slicing.

Per serving: Calories 243, Protein 4 g, Fat 9 g, Carbohydrate 40 g, Fiber 6 g, Sodium 229 mg

Cookies

Wheat-Free Almond Jam Dots

☆ ☆

Makes 1½ dozen cookies

This simple and wonderful cookie was adapted from a recipe from the Natural Gourmet Cookery School in New York City.

½ cup maple syrup

½ cup canola, safflower, or sunflower oil

½ teaspoon vanilla

1 teaspoon almond extract

1 cup almonds, roasted and cooled (page 101)

1 cup rolled oats

1 cup barley flour

¼ teaspoon ground cinnamon

½ teaspoon salt

3 tablespoons jam or fruit preserves

Preheat the oven to 350°F. In a small bowl, mix the syrup, oil, vanilla, and almond extract; set aside.

Process the almonds, oats, flour, cinnamon, and salt in a food processor or blender until they are the consistency of fine meal. (Be sure the almonds are completely cooled before processing; otherwise, you will end up with a pasty mess.) Transfer the oat mixture to a large bowl. Pour the wet ingredients into the dry ingredients, and mix with a spatula until everything is well incorporated.

With a 1-ounce ice cream scoop or 2 spoons, scoop out 1 heaping tablespoon of the batter onto well-oiled or parchment-lined cookie sheets. Flatten the cookies slightly with the bottom of a cup or glass. (Dip the bottom of the cup or glass in warm water before flattening each cookie. The water will prevent the batter from sticking.)

With the back of a 1-teaspoon measuring spoon, make an indentation in the top of each cookie. (Dip the spoon into warm water to prevent the batter from sticking.) Place ½ teaspoon of the jam or preserves into the indentation of each cookie.

Bake for 12 minutes and rotate the cookie sheets a half turn to ensure even baking. Bake 5 to 7 minutes more or until the cookies are golden around the edges. Let cool on the cookie sheets 5 to 6 minutes and then remove to a cooling rack.

Per cookie: Calories 176, Protein 3 g, Fat 11 g, Carbohydrate 18 g, Fiber 3 g, Sodium 63 mg

Peanut Butter & Jelly Thumbprints

☆ ☆

This is like having all of the comforts of childhood in a tiny little cookie. These cookies not only look beautiful, but the taste is amazingly familiar.

½ cup maple syrup

½ cup canola, safflower, or sunflower oil

½ teaspoon vanilla

1 cup roasted peanuts (page 101)

¾ cup rolled oats

1 cup barley flour

½ teaspoon salt

½ teaspoon baking soda

½ teaspoon baking powder

3 tablespoons grape jelly

Preheat the oven to 350°F. In a small bowl, mix the syrup, oil, and vanilla; set aside. Process the peanuts and oats in a food processor or blender until they are the consistency of fine meal. (Be sure the peanuts are completely cooled before processing; otherwise, you will end up with a pasty mess.)

In a separate, larger bowl, sift the flour, salt, baking soda, and baking powder. (Sifting isn't absolutely necessary, but it ensures there won't be clumps of flour or salt in the batter.) Add the nut-oat mixture. Pour the wet ingredients into the dry ingredients, and mix with a spatula until everything is well incorporated.

With a 1-ounce ice cream scoop or 2 spoons, scoop out 1 heaping tablespoon of the batter onto well-oiled or parchment-lined cookie sheets. Flatten the cookies slightly with the bottom of a cup or glass. (Dip the bottom of the cup or glass in warm water before flattening each cookie. The water will prevent the batter from sticking.)

With your thumb or the back of a 1-teaspoon measuring spoon, make an indentation in the top of each cookie. (Dip the spoon into warm water to prevent the batter from sticking.) Place ½ teaspoon of the jelly into the indentation of each cookie.

Bake for 11 minutes and rotate the cookie sheets a half turn to ensure even baking. Bake 4 to 5 minutes more or until the cookies are golden around the edges. Let cool on the cookie sheets 5 to 6 minutes and then remove to a cooling rack.

Per cookie: Calories 120, Protein 3 g, Fat 5 g, Carbohydrate 17 g, Fiber 2 g, Sodium 108 mg

Almond Shortbread Cookies

☆ ☆

Makes 2 dozen cookies

These little tea cookies are perfectly sweet with a wonderful crunch. They are fantastic right out of the oven or savored slowly with a hot cup of herbal tea.

Topping:

1 teaspoon barley flour

2 teaspoons maple sugar, Sucanat, or date sugar

Shortbread:

1 cup roasted almonds (page 101)

¾ cup rolled oats

½ cup canola, safflower, or sunflower oil

½ cup maple syrup

½ teaspoon vanilla

1 cup barley flour

½ teaspoon baking soda

½ teaspoon baking powder

½ teaspoon salt

¼ teaspoon ground cinnamon

Preheat the oven to 350°F. In a small bowl, mix topping ingredients; set aside. Process the almonds and oats in a food processor or blender until they are the consistency of coarse flour; transfer to a large bowl and set aside.

In another small bowl, mix the oil, syrup, and vanilla; set aside.

Sift the remaining dry ingredients into the nut-oat mixture. (Sifting isn't absolutely necessary, but it ensures there won't be clumps of flour or salt in the batter.) Pour the wet ingredients into the dry ingredients, and mix with a spatula until everything is well incorporated.

With a 1-ounce ice cream scoop or 2 spoons, scoop out 1 heaping tablespoon of the batter onto well-oiled or parchment-lined cookie sheets. Flatten the cookies slightly with the bottom of a cup or glass. (Dip the bottom of the cup or glass in warm water before flattening each cookie to prevent the batter from sticking.) Sprinkle each cookie with topping.

Bake for 11 minutes and rotate the cookie sheets a half turn to ensure even baking. Bake 4 to 5 minutes more or until the cookies are golden around the edges. Let cool on the cookie sheets 5 to 6 minutes and then remove to a cooling rack.

 Per cookie: Calories 124, Protein 2 g, Fat 8 g, Carbohydrate 11 g, Fiber 2 g, Sodium 80 mg

Cashew Jam Bites

☆ *Makes about 4 dozen cookies*

This cookie is the perfect tea cookie—elegant, light, and crispy. The cashews lend a wonderful buttery quality. The jam tastes fabulous, but you can omit it and prepare this as a drop cookie.

Topping:

1 teaspoon maple sugar, Sucanat, or date sugar

1/4 teaspoon nutmeg

Cookies:

1 cup roasted cashews (page 101)

3/4 cup rolled oats

1/2 cup canola, safflower, or sunflower oil

1/2 cup maple syrup

1/2 teaspoon vanilla

1 cup barley flour

1/2 teaspoon baking soda

1/2 teaspoon baking powder

1/2 teaspoon salt

Dash of grated nutmeg

3 tablespoons jam or fruit preserves

Preheat the oven to 350°F. In a small bowl, mix the topping ingredients; set aside. Process the cashews and oats in a food processor or blender until they are the consistency of coarse flour; transfer to a large bowl and set aside. In a small bowl, mix the oil, syrup, and vanilla; set aside.

Sift the flour, baking soda, baking powder, salt, and nutmeg into the nut-oat mixture. (Sifting isn't absolutely necessary, but it ensures there won't be clumps of flour or salt in the batter.) Pour the wet ingredients into the dry ingredients, and mix with a spatula until everything is well incorporated.

With a 1-ounce ice cream scoop or 2 spoons, scoop out 1 heaping tablespoon of the batter onto well-oiled or parchment-lined cookie sheets. Flatten the cookies slightly with the bottom of a cup or glass. (Dip the bottom of the cup or glass in warm water before flattening each cookie. The water will prevent the batter from sticking.)

With the back of a 1-teaspoon measuring spoon, make an indentation in the top of each cookie. (Dip the spoon into warm water to prevent the batter from sticking.) Place 1/2 teaspoon of the jam or preserves into the indentation of each cookie. Sprinkle each cookie with topping.

Bake for 11 minutes and rotate the cookie sheets a half turn to ensure even baking. Bake 4 to 5 minutes more or until the cookies are golden around the edges. Let cool on the cookie sheets 5 to 6 minutes and then remove to a cooling rack.

Per serving: Calories 64, Protein 1 g, Fat 4 g, Carbohydrate 7 g, Fiber 0.6 g, Sodium 41 mg

Oatmeal Raisin Cookies

☆   Makes 1½ dozen cookies

Looking to take a break from chocolate? If you love the old-fashioned flavors of oatmeal and cinnamon together, this is your cookie. Filled with raisins and walnuts, this cookie is just delicious. The oats give this cookie great texture, and the spices tie it all together.

1½ cups rolled oats, divided

¼ cup plus 2 tablespoons canola, safflower, or sunflower oil

½ cup plus 2 tablespoons maple syrup

½ teaspoons vanilla

¾ cup raisins

¼ cup chopped walnuts (optional)

1 cup barley flour

½ teaspoon baking soda

½ teaspoon baking powder

¼ teaspoon ground cinnamon

Dash of grated nutmeg

½ teaspoon salt

Preheat the oven to 350°F. Process ¾ cup of the oats in a food processor or blender until they are the consistency of coarse flour; set aside. In a small bowl, mix the oil, syrup, and vanilla; set aside.

In a separate, larger bowl, place the ground oats, remaining ¾ cup rolled oats, raisins, and walnuts, if using. Sift the flour, baking soda, baking powder, spices, and salt into the oat mixture. (Sifting isn't absolutely necessary, but it ensures there won't be clumps of flour or salt in the batter.) Pour the wet ingredients into the dry ingredients, and mix with a spatula until everything is well incorporated.

With a 1-ounce ice cream scoop or 2 spoons, scoop out 1 heaping tablespoon of the batter onto well-oiled or parchment-lined cookie sheets. Flatten the cookies slightly with the bottom of a cup or glass. (Dip the bottom of the cup or glass in warm water before flattening each cookie. The water will prevent the batter from sticking.)

Bake for 11 minutes and rotate the cookie sheets a half turn to ensure even baking. Bake 6 to 7 minutes more or until the cookies are golden around the edges. Let cool on the cookie sheets 5 to 6 minutes and then remove to a cooling rack.

For Oatmeal Chocolate Chip Cookies

Substitute 1 cup chocolate chips for the raisins.

Per cookie: Calories 137, Protein 2 g, Fat 5 g, Carbohydrate 22 g, Fiber 2 g, Sodium 107 mg

Mint Double Carob Walnut Cookies

☆ ☆

Makes 1½ dozen cookies

These cookies are rich and decidedly decadent. The carob flavor is enhanced by the refreshing taste of peppermint and walnuts.

¾ cup rolled oats

¼ cup plus 2 tablespoons canola, safflower, or sunflower oil

½ cup plus 2 tablespoons maple syrup

1 tablespoon peppermint extract

½ teaspoon vanilla

½ cup Sucanat, date sugar, or maple sugar

½ cup vegan carob chips

1 cup roughly chopped walnuts (almost whole pieces)

1 cup barley flour

½ cup plus 1 tablespoon lightly roasted carob powder

½ teaspoon baking powder

½ teaspoon salt

Preheat the oven to 350°F. Process the oats in a food processor or blender until they are the consistency of coarse flour; set aside. In a small bowl, mix the oil, syrup, peppermint extract, and vanilla; set aside.

In a separate, larger bowl, mix the ground oats, Sucanat, carob chips, and walnuts. Sift the flour, carob powder, baking powder, and salt into the oat mixture. (Sifting isn't absolutely necessary, but it ensures there won't be clumps of flour or salt in the batter.) Pour the wet ingredients into the dry ingredients, and mix with a spatula until everything is well incorporated.

With a 1-ounce ice cream scoop or 2 spoons, scoop out 1 heaping tablespoon of the batter onto well-oiled or parchment-lined cookie sheets. Flatten the cookies slightly with the bottom of a cup or glass. (Dip the bottom of the cup or glass in warm water before flattening each cookie. The water will prevent the batter from sticking.)

Bake for 11 minutes and rotate the cookie sheets a half turn to ensure even baking. Bake 5 minutes more or until cookies are golden around the edges. Let cool on the cookie sheets 5 to 6 minutes and then remove to a cooling rack.

For a chocolate version

Use chocolate chips and cocoa powder in place of the carob chips and carob powder.

Per cookie: Calories 195, Protein 3 g, Fat 10 g, Carbohydrate 26 g, Fiber 2 g, Sodium 72 mg

Chocolate Spiral Cookies

☆ ☆

These are amazingly lovely cookies, much like a chocolate Oreo but with a little more flair. Vary the size by simply making larger or smaller spirals. These cookies take a little preparation, but they are well worth it.

Chocolate Crème Filling:

8 ounces firm or extra-firm tofu

1 cup chocolate chips

½ cup soymilk or cashew milk

1 tablespoon maple syrup

1 tablespoon vanilla

⅛ teaspoon salt

In a pot of boiling water, blanch the tofu for 5 minutes; drain. Set aside. (Blanching removes the bean-y flavor and results in a creamier texture.)

Melt the chocolate chips in the top of a double boiler or in a metal bowl over a pot of boiling water. (Note: Be careful to keep moisture out of the chocolate to prevent seizing, in which the chocolate becomes a solid, grainy mass that will not melt.)

When the chocolate is almost melted, break up the tofu into large chunks and process it in a food processor or blender for 2 minutes. (This helps remove the gritty texture from the tofu and results in a really smooth cream.)

Add the melted chocolate and the remaining ingredients, and process until well incorporated, occasionally scraping down the sides of the bowl with a spatula. When it is completely smooth, strain the mixture through a sieve or a very fine mesh strainer into a shallow dish. Refrigerate at least 4 to 5 hours until mixture has set up and become firm.

☆ ☆

Cookies:

¼ cup plus 2 tablespoons canola, safflower, or sunflower oil

½ cup plus 2 tablespoons maple syrup

½ teaspoon vanilla

¼ cup Sucanat, date sugar, or maple sugar

1½ cups barley flour

½ teaspoon baking powder

½ teaspoon salt

¼ cup cocoa powder

⅛ teaspoon ground cinnamon

Preheat the oven to 350°F. In a small bowl, mix the oil, syrup, and vanilla.

In a separate, larger bowl, pour in the Sucanat; sift all of the remaining ingredients into the bowl with the Sucanat. (Sifting isn't absolutely necessary, but it ensures there won't be clumps of flour or salt in the batter.) Pour the wet ingredients into the dry ingredients, and mix with a spatula until everything is well incorporated.

Place the batter in a pastry bag fitted with a very large tip. Squeeze the batter into round spirals onto parchment-lined cookie sheets.

Bake for 11 minutes and rotate the cookie sheets a half turn to ensure even baking. Bake 4 to 5 minutes more or until the cookies are crisp around the edges. Let the cookies cool 5 minutes, and then cool them completely on a wire rack before assembling the sandwiches.

Bring the Chocolate Crème Filling to room temperature, and place in a pastry bag fitted with a medium tip. Squeeze the filling into round spirals onto the flat side of a cookie. Alternatively, spoon the filling onto the flat side of a cookie and spread it with a spoon. Top it with the flat side of another cookie. Repeat until you've used all of the remaining cookies and filling.

 Per cookie: Calories 268, Protein 5 g, Fat 13 g, Carbohydrate 37 g, Fiber 4 g, Sodium 130 mg

Cashew or Pecan Sandies

☆ ☆

Makes 18 cookies

This cookie has a wonderful light texture. The cashews have a buttery flavor that is just wonderful in this recipe. Substitute pecans if you prefer.

½ cup maple syrup

½ teaspoon vanilla

1 cup barley flour

1 cup roasted cashews or pecans
   (page 101)

¾ cup rolled oats

½ teaspoon baking soda

½ teaspoon baking powder

½ teaspoon salt

½ cup canola, safflower, or sunflower oil,
   placed in the freezer for 15 minutes

18 whole cashews or pecans (optional)

Preheat the oven to 350°F. In a small bowl, mix the syrup and vanilla; set aside. Process the flour, nuts, oats, baking soda, baking powder, and salt in a food processor or blender until they are the consistency of fine meal.

Add the cold oil and process until the mixture looks like sand. With the machine running, add the syrup and vanilla mixture.

With a 1-ounce ice cream scoop or 2 spoons, scoop out 1 heaping tablespoon of the batter onto well-oiled or parchment-lined cookie sheets. Flatten the cookies slightly with the bottom of a cup or glass. (Dip the bottom of the cup or glass in warm water before flattening each cookie. The water will prevent the batter from sticking.)

Using a fork dipped in warm water, make a crisscross pattern on the top of each cookie. Place 1 whole cashew on top of each cookie, if desired. Bake for 11 minutes and rotate the cookie sheets a half turn to ensure even baking. Bake 4 to 5 minutes more or until the cookies are golden around the edges. Let cool on the cookie sheets 5 to 6 minutes and then remove to a cooling rack.

 Per cookie: Calories 162, Protein 3 g, Fat 10 g, Carbohydrate 16 g, Fiber 2 g, Sodium 107 mg

Cornmeal Sandies

☆ ☆

Makes about 18 cookies

Cornmeal adds a whole new dimension in taste and texture to cookies. This cookie is a symphony of great flavors but is SO simple to make.

½ cup roasted pecans (page 101), divided

½ cup roasted almonds (page 101), divided

1 cup barley flour

½ cup cornmeal

½ cup rolled oats

½ teaspoon baking soda

½ teaspoon baking powder

½ teaspoon salt

½ cup canola, safflower, or sunflower oil

½ cup maple syrup

½ teaspoon almond extract

½ teaspoon vanilla

Preheat the oven to 350°F. Coarsely chop ¼ cup of the pecans and ¼ cup of the almonds; set aside.

Process the flour, remaining pecans and almonds, cornmeal, oats, baking soda, baking powder, and salt in a food processor or blender until they are the consistency of coarse meal. Transfer this mixture to a large bowl, and set aside.

In a small bowl, mix the oil, syrup, almond extract, and vanilla. Pour the wet ingredients into the dry ingredients, and mix with a spatula until everything is well incorporated.

With a 1-ounce ice cream scoop or 2 spoons, scoop out 1 heaping tablespoon of the batter onto well-oiled or parchment-lined cookie sheets. Flatten the cookies slightly with the bottom of a cup or glass. (Dip the bottom of the cup or glass in warm water before flattening each cookie. The water will prevent the batter from sticking.)

Bake for 11 minutes and rotate the cookie sheets a half turn to ensure even baking. Bake 6 to 7 minutes more or until the cookies are golden around the edges. Let cool on the cookie sheets 5 to 6 minutes and then remove to a cooling rack.

Per cookie: Calories 167, Protein 2 g, Fat 11 g, Carbohydrate 16 g, Fiber 2 g, Sodium 107 mg

Double Fudge Pecan Brownies

☆ ☆

Makes six 2 to 3" brownies

I began formulating these lovely chocolate dreams when I was still in school. They underwent a few makeovers until it was agreed: This is the recipe. Sweet potatoes give this brownie great texture and an intensely rich flavor. They are amazing on their own or with a scoop of your favorite vanilla "ice cream." I love them ice cold.

⅓ cup rolled oats

¼ cup plus 1 tablespoon Sweet Potato Purée (page 41)

¼ cup maple syrup

¼ cup canola, safflower, or sunflower oil

1 tablespoon vanilla

¾ cup Sucanat, date sugar, or maple sugar

¼ cup chocolate chips*

¼ cup pecans, divided (optional)

⅓ cup barley flour*

½ cup cocoa powder

¼ teaspoon baking powder

Heaping ¼ teaspoon salt

(*You can use carob powder and vegan carob chips in place of the cocoa powder and chocolate chips.)

Preheat the oven to 350°F. Oil an 8 x 8" baking pan. Process the oats in a food processor or blender until they are the consistency of coarse flour. In a small bowl, mix the sweet potato purée, syrup, oil, and vanilla.

In a separate, larger bowl, mix the ground oats, Sucanat, chocolate chips, and half of the pecans, if using. Sift the flour, cocoa, baking powder, and salt into the oat mixture. (Sifting isn't absolutely necessary, but it ensures there won't be clumps of flour or salt in the batter.) Pour the wet ingredients into the dry ingredients, and mix with a spatula until everything is well incorporated.

Pour the batter into the prepared pan. Sprinkle with the remaining pecans. Bake 20 minutes and rotate the pan a half turn to ensure even baking. Bake 10 to 13 minutes more or until a knife inserted in the center comes out clean. Let cool at least 30 minutes before cutting.

For Double Fudge Walnut Brownies

Use walnuts instead of pecans.

For Mint Double Fudge Brownies

Add 1 teaspoon peppermint extract.

For Mocha Fudge Brownies

Add ¼ cup coffee substitute powder or granules.

For Double Fudge Orange Brownies

Add the juice and zest of ¼ orange.

Per brownie: Calories 230, Protein 3 g, Fat 3 g, Carbohydrate 52 g, Fiber 4 g, Sodium 108 mg

Almond Butter Cookies

☆ ☆

Makes 2 dozen cookies

These cookies are a twist on our peanut butter cookie. For those who desire a new and different taste, this cookie is equally rich. They're wonderful with chocolate chips or vegan carob chips.

³/₄ cup rolled oats

1 cup crunchy almond butter

½ cup plus 2 tablespoons maple syrup

¼ cup plus 2 tablespoons canola, safflower, or sunflower oil

½ teaspoon vanilla

³/₄ cup chocolate chips (optional)

³/₄ cup barley flour

½ teaspoon baking soda

½ teaspoon baking powder

½ teaspoon salt

Preheat the oven to 350°F. Process the oats in a food processor or blender until they are the consistency of coarse flour. In a small bowl, mix the almond butter, syrup, oil, and vanilla.

In a separate, larger bowl, mix the ground oats and chocolate chips, if using. Sift the flour, baking soda, baking powder, and salt into the oat mixture. (Sifting isn't absolutely necessary, but it ensures there won't be clumps of flour or salt in the batter.) Pour the wet ingredients into the dry ingredients, and mix with a spatula until everything is well incorporated.

With a 1-ounce ice cream scoop or 2 spoons, scoop out 1 heaping tablespoon of the batter onto well-oiled or parchment-lined cookie sheets.

Bake for 11 minutes and rotate the cookie sheets a half turn to ensure even baking. Bake 6 to 7 minutes more or until the cookies are golden around the edges. Let cool on the cookie sheets 5 to 6 minutes and then remove to a cooling rack.

For Cashew Butter Cookies

Substitute cashew butter for the almond butter.

Per cookie: Calories 135, Protein 3 g, Fat 9 g, Carbohydrate 11 g, Fiber 1 g, Sodium 91 mg

Clove Cookies

☆ ☆

Makes 2½ dozen cookies

Although the aroma of ground cloves is reminiscent of the holiday season, these cookies are wonderful any time of the year. Dusted with a maple-clove topping, they easily share in holiday fare, but are lovely for any occasion.

¼ cup rolled oats

¼ cup plus 2 teaspoons canola, safflower, or sunflower oil

½ cup plus 2 teaspoons maple syrup

1 teaspoon vanilla

1¼ cups barley flour

½ teaspoon baking soda

½ teaspoon baking powder

½ teaspoon salt

2 teaspoons ground cloves

1 teaspoon ground cinnamon

Topping:

1 teaspoon barley flour

2 teaspoons maple sugar, Sucanat, or date sugar

¼ teaspoon ground cloves

Preheat the oven to 350°F. Process the oats in a food processor or blender until they are the consistency of coarse flour. In a small bowl, mix the oil, syrup, and vanilla; set aside.

In a separate, larger bowl, place the ground oats. Sift the flour, baking soda, baking powder, salt, cloves, and cinnamon into the ground oats. (Sifting isn't absolutely necessary, but it ensures there won't be clumps of flour or salt in the batter.) Pour the wet ingredients into the dry ingredients and mix with a spatula until everything is well incorporated.

With a 1-ounce ice cream scoop or 2 spoons, scoop out 1 heaping tablespoon of the batter onto well-oiled or parchment-lined cookie sheets. Flatten the cookies slightly with the bottom of a cup or glass. (Dip the bottom of the cup or glass in warm water before flattening each cookie to prevent the batter from sticking to the glass.)

In a small bowl, mix the topping ingredients. Sprinkle each cookie with topping.

Bake for 11 minutes and rotate the cookie sheets a half turn to ensure even baking. Bake 4 to 5 minutes more or until the cookies are golden around the edges. Let cool on the cookie sheets 5 to 6 minutes and then remove to a cooling rack.

Per cookie: Calories 55, Protein 1 g, Fat 2 g, Carbohydrate 8 g, Fiber 1 g, Sodium 63 mg

Lemon Ginger Snaps

☆ ☆

Lemon and ginger, always a wonderful combination, provide a punchy zip and a wonderful lemon essence to these crisp and light cookies. They are truly delightful and refreshing.

Topping:

1 tablespoon barley flour

2 tablespoons maple sugar, Sucanat, or date sugar

Cookies:

1/4 cup rolled oats

1/4 cup plus 2 tablespoons canola, safflower, or sunflower oil

1/2 cup plus 2 tablespoons maple syrup

1/2 teaspoon vanilla

1 tablespoon grated fresh ginger or 1/2 teaspoon powdered ginger

1 tablespoon lemon zest

1 1/4 cups barley flour

1/4 teaspoon baking soda

1/4 teaspoon baking powder

1 tablespoon lemon powder* or lemon extract

1/2 teaspoon salt

*See Sources (pages 121-22) to purchase lemon powder.

Preheat the oven to 350°F. In a small bowl, mix the topping ingredients; set aside. Process the oats in a food processor or blender until they are the consistency of coarse flour. In a small bowl, mix the oil, syrup, vanilla, and fresh ginger, if using.

In a separate, larger bowl, place the ground oats and the zest. Sift the flour, baking soda, baking powder, ground ginger, if using, lemon powder, and salt into the oat mixture. (Sifting isn't absolutely necessary, but it ensures there won't be clumps of flour or salt in the batter.) Pour the wet ingredients into the dry ingredients and mix with a spatula until everything is well incorporated.

With a 1-ounce ice cream scoop or 2 spoons, scoop out 1 heaping tablespoon of the batter onto well-oiled or parchment-lined cookie sheets. Flatten the cookies slightly with the bottom of a cup or glass. (Dip the bottom of the cup or glass in warm water before flattening each cookie to prevent the batter from sticking to the glass.) Sprinkle each cookie with topping.

Bake for 11 minutes and rotate the cookie sheets a half turn to ensure even baking. Bake 5 to 6 minutes more or until the cookies are golden around the edges. Let cool on the cookie sheets for 5 to 6 minutes before removing to a cooling rack.

For Lemon Poppy Seed Cookies

Omit the lemon powder. Add 1 tablespoon poppy seeds and 2 teaspoons lemon extract.

Per cookie: Calories 54, Protein 1 g, Fat 2 g, Carbohydrate 7 g, Fiber 1 g, Sodium 42 mg

Ginger Snaps

☆ ☆

Makes 3 dozen cookies

These cookies have a wonderful crunch, packed with the intense flavor of ginger.

Topping:

1 teaspoon barley flour

2 teaspoons maple sugar, Sucanat, or date sugar

Cookies:

1/2 cup rolled oats, divided

1/4 cup plus 2 tablespoons canola, safflower, or sunflower oil

1/2 cup maple syrup

2 tablespoons blackstrap molasses

1/2 teaspoon vanilla

1 cup plus 2 tablespoons barley flour

1/2 teaspoon baking soda

1/2 teaspoon baking powder

1/2 teaspoon salt

1 1/2 teaspoons powdered ginger

1/2 teaspoon ground cinnamon

Preheat the oven to 350°F. In a small bowl, mix the topping ingredients; set aside. Process 1/4 cup of the oats in a food processor or blender until they are the consistency of coarse flour. In a small bowl, mix the oil, syrup, molasses, and vanilla.

In a separate, larger bowl, place the ground oats and remaining rolled oats. Sift the flour, baking soda, baking powder, salt, ginger, and cinnamon into the oats. (Sifting isn't absolutely necessary, but it ensures there won't be clumps of flour or salt in the batter.) Pour the wet ingredients into the dry ingredients, and mix with a spatula until everything is well incorporated.

With a 1-ounce ice cream scoop or 2 spoons, scoop out 1 heaping tablespoon of the batter onto well-oiled or parchment-lined cookie sheets. Sprinkle each cookie with topping.

Bake for 10 minutes and rotate the cookie sheets a half turn to ensure even baking. Bake 6 to 7 minutes more or until the cookies are golden around the edges. Let cool on the cookie sheets for 5 to 6 minutes before removing to a cooling rack.

For Cinnamon Snaps

Add 1 teaspoon ground cinnamon to the topping mixture. Substitute 2 teaspoons cinnamon for the powdered ginger. Add 2 tablespoons maple syrup.

Per cookie: Calories 53, Protein 1 g, Fat 2 g, Carbohydrate 7 g, Fiber 1 g, Sodium 53 mg

Gingerbread Cookies

☆ ☆

Makes 3 dozen cookies

This is another lovely holiday cookie. Filled with aromatic spices, ginger, and cinnamon, these are a wonderful accompaniment to a cup of hot tea.

Topping:

1 teaspoon barley flour

2 tablespoons maple sugar, Sucanat, or date sugar

Cookies:

¼ cup rolled oats

¼ cup plus 2 tablespoons canola, safflower, or sunflower oil

½ cup maple syrup

2 tablespoons blackstrap molasses

½ teaspoon vanilla

½ cup raisins

1¼ cups barley flour

½ teaspoon baking soda

½ teaspoon baking powder

1½ teaspoons powdered ginger

½ teaspoon cinnamon

½ teaspoon salt

Preheat the oven to 350°F. In a small bowl, mix the topping ingredients; set aside. Process the oats in a food processor or blender until they are the consistency of coarse flour. In a small bowl, mix the oil, syrup, molasses, and vanilla.

In a separate, larger bowl, place the ground oats and the raisins. Sift the flour, baking soda, baking powder, ginger, cinnamon, and salt into the oat mixture. (Sifting isn't absolutely necessary, but it ensures there won't be clumps of flour or salt in the batter.) Pour the wet ingredients into the dry ingredients, and mix with a spatula until everything is well incorporated.

With a 1-ounce ice cream scoop or 2 spoons, scoop out 1 heaping tablespoon of the batter onto well-oiled or parchment-lined cookie sheets. Sprinkle each cookie with topping.

Bake for 10 minutes and rotate the cookie sheets a half turn to ensure even baking. Bake 4 to 5 minutes more or until the cookies are golden around the edges. Let cool on the cookie sheets for 5 to 6 minutes before removing to a cooling rack.

Per cookie: Calories 57, Protein 1 g, Fat 2 g, Carbohydrate 9 g, Fiber 1 g, Sodium 54 mg

Coconut Macaroons

☆ ☆

Makes 18 cookies

These cookies are simply wonderful and quick and easy to make.

¼ cup plus 1 tablespoon barley flour

¼ teaspoon baking soda

¼ teaspoon baking powder

¼ teaspoon salt

2½ cups shredded, toasted coconut (see below)

8 pitted dates

½ cup Sucanat, date sugar, or maple sugar

5 tablespoons water

Preheat the oven to 350°F. Sift the flour, baking soda, baking powder, and salt into the bowl of a food processor or blender. (Sifting isn't absolutely necessary, but it ensures there won't be clumps of flour or salt in the batter.) Add the coconut, dates, and Sucanat to the flour mixture. Process until the dates are chopped and the mixture comes together. With the machine running, add the water through the top; process until a dough forms.

With a 1-ounce ice cream scoop or 2 spoons, scoop out 1 heaping tablespoon of the batter onto well-oiled or parchment-lined cookie sheets. Flatten the cookies slightly with the bottom of a cup or glass. (Dip the bottom of the cup or glass in warm water before flattening each cookie to prevent the batter from sticking to the glass.)

With a fork dipped in warm water, press around the edges of each cookie, creating a fluted edge. Bake for 11 minutes and rotate the cookie sheets a half turn to ensure even baking. Bake 5 to 6 minutes more or until the cookies are golden around the edges. Let cool on the cookie sheets for 5 to 6 minutes before removing to a cooling rack.

To toast coconut

If using raw, shredded coconut, place on a parchment-lined cookie sheet, and bake at 350°F for 10 to 12 minutes or until the coconut begins to turn golden brown. Let cool completely, about 10 minutes.

Per serving: Calories 245, Protein 2 g, Fat 20 g, Carbohydrate 17 g, Fiber 6 g, Sodium 230 mg

Coconut Chocolate Chews

☆ ☆

Makes 18 cookies

These cookies are absolutely AWESOME. They are moist, chocolaty, chewy, a chocolate lover's dream. They are so easy to prepare but look and taste absolutely decadent.

½ cup cocoa or carob powder

¼ cup barley flour

¼ teaspoon baking soda

¼ teaspoon baking powder

¼ teaspoon salt

2½ cups shredded, toasted coconut (see below)

8 pitted dates

1 cup Sucanat, date sugar, or maple sugar

5 tablespoons water

Preheat the oven to 350°F. Sift the cocoa or carob powder, flour, baking soda, baking powder, and salt into the bowl of a food processor or blender. (Sifting isn't absolutely necessary, but it ensures there won't be clumps of flour or salt in the batter.) Add the coconut, dates, and Sucanat to the flour mixture. Process until the dates are chopped and the mixture comes together. With the machine running, add the water through the top; process until a dough forms.

With a 1-ounce ice cream scoop or 2 spoons, scoop out 1 heaping tablespoon of the batter onto well-oiled or parchment-lined cookie sheets. Flatten the cookies slightly with the bottom of a cup or glass. (Dip the bottom of the cup or glass in warm water before flattening each cookie to prevent the batter from sticking to the glass.)

With a fork dipped in warm water, press around the edges of each cookie, creating a fluted edge. Bake for 11 minutes and rotate the cookie sheets a half turn to ensure even baking. Bake 5 to 6 minutes more or until the cookies are golden around the edges. Let cool on the cookie sheets for 5 to 6 minutes before removing to a cooling rack.

To toast coconut

If using raw, shredded coconut, place on a parchment-lined cookie sheet, and bake at 350°F for 10 to 12 minutes or until the coconut begins to turn golden brown. Let cool completely, about 10 minutes.

Per cookie: Calories 269, Protein 3 g, Fat 21 g, Carbohydrate 24 g, Fiber 7 g, Sodium 64 mg

Tahini Chocolate Chip Cookies

☆☆☆☆☆☆☆☆☆☆☆☆☆☆☆☆☆☆☆☆☆☆☆☆

Makes 2 dozen cookies

This is an interesting, rich and buttery cookie combining tahini—a nutty-flavored paste of ground sesame seeds—and peanut butter. Use the roasted tahini if possible for the most flavor. My dad loves them.

¾ cup rolled oats

½ cup tahini

¼ cup peanut butter

¼ cup plus 2 tablespoons canola, safflower, or sunflower oil

½ cup plus 2 tablespoons maple syrup

½ teaspoon vanilla

¾ cup chocolate chips (optional)

¾ cup barley flour

½ teaspoon baking soda

½ teaspoon baking powder

½ teaspoon salt

Preheat the oven to 350°F. Process the oats in a food processor or blender until they are the consistency of coarse flour. In a small bowl, mix the tahini, peanut butter, oil, syrup, and vanilla; set aside.

In a separate, larger bowl, mix the ground oats and chocolate chips, if using. Sift the flour, baking soda, baking powder, and salt into the oat mixture. (Sifting isn't absolutely necessary, but it ensures there won't be clumps of flour or salt in the batter.) Pour the wet ingredients into the dry ingredients, and mix with a spatula until everything is well incorporated.

With a 1-ounce ice cream scoop or 2 spoons, scoop out 1 heaping tablespoon of the batter onto well-oiled or parchment-lined cookie sheets. Flatten the cookies slightly with the bottom of a cup or glass. (Dip the bottom of the cup or glass in warm water before flattening each cookie to prevent the batter from sticking to the glass.) Using a fork dipped in warm water, make a criss-cross pattern on the top of each cookie.

Bake for 11 minutes and rotate the cookie sheets a half turn to ensure even baking. Bake 6 to 7 minutes more or until the cookies are golden around the edges. Let cool on the cookie sheets for 5 to 6 minutes before removing to a cooling rack.

Per cookie: Calories 120, Protein 2 g, Fat 7 g, Carbohydrate 12 g, Fiber 1.5 g, Sodium 89 mg

Soy Nut Butter Chocolate Chip Cookies

☆ ☆

Makes 2 dozen cookies

These cookies have the added benefit of whole soy protein and are super yummy.

3/4 cup rolled oats

1/4 cup plus 2 tablespoons canola, safflower, or sunflower oil

1/2 cup plus 2 tablespoons maple syrup

1 cup crunchy soy nut butter

1/2 teaspoon vanilla

1 cup chocolate chips (optional)

1 cup barley flour

1/2 teaspoon baking soda

1/2 teaspoon baking powder

1/2 teaspoon salt

Preheat the oven to 350°F. Process the oats in a food processor or blender until they are the consistency of coarse flour. In a small bowl, mix the oil, syrup, soy nut butter, and vanilla.

In a separate, larger bowl, mix the ground oats and the chocolate chips, if using. Sift the flour, baking soda, baking powder, and salt into the oat mixture. (Sifting isn't absolutely necessary, but it ensures there won't be clumps of flour or salt in the batter.) Pour the wet ingredients into the dry ingredients, and mix with a spatula until everything is well incorporated.

With a 1-ounce ice cream scoop or 2 spoons, scoop out 1 heaping tablespoon of the batter onto well-oiled or parchment-lined cookie sheets. Dip a fork in warm water and make a criss-cross pattern on the top of each cookie.

Bake for 11 minutes and rotate the cookie sheets a half turn to ensure even baking. Bake 6 to 7 minutes more or until the cookies are golden around the edges. Let cool on the cookie sheets 5 to 6 minutes and then remove to a cooling rack.

Per cookie: Calories 136, Protein 4 g, Fat 7 g, Carbohydrate 14 g, Fiber 1 g, Sodium 136 mg

Chocolate-Chocolate Macadamia Nut Cookies

☆   Makes 2 dozen cookies

Jill once had a dream about a chocolate cookie with macadamia nuts. Here they are: rich with intense cocoa flavor, dark chocolate chips, and buttery macadamia nuts.

¾ cup rolled oats

½ cup plus 2 tablespoons maple syrup

¼ cup plus 2 tablespoons canola, safflower, or sunflower oil

½ teaspoon vanilla

¾ cup chocolate chips

¾ cup roughly chopped macadamia nuts

1 cup barley flour

½ cup plus 1 tablespoon cocoa powder

½ cup Sucanat, date sugar, or maple sugar

½ teaspoon baking powder

½ teaspoon salt

Preheat the oven to 350°F. Process the oats in a food processor or blender until they are the consistency of coarse flour. In a small bowl, mix the syrup, oil, and vanilla; set aside.

In a separate, larger bowl, mix the ground oats, chocolate chips, and nuts. Sift the flour, cocoa, Sucanat, baking powder, and salt into the oat flour mixture. (Sifting isn't absolutely necessary, but it ensures there won't be clumps of flour or salt in the batter.) Pour the wet ingredients into the dry ingredients, and mix with a spatula until everything is well incorporated.

With a 1-ounce ice cream scoop or 2 spoons, scoop out 1 heaping tablespoon of the batter onto well-oiled or parchment-lined cookie sheets. Flatten the cookies slightly with the bottom of a cup or glass. (Dip the bottom of the cup or glass in warm water before flattening each cookie to prevent the batter from sticking to the glass.)

Bake for 11 minutes and rotate the cookie sheets a half turn to ensure even baking. Bake 5 minutes more or until the cookies are crisp around the edges. Let cool on the cookie sheets for 5 to 6 minutes before removing to a cooling rack.

For a chocolate-free alternative

Replace the cocoa powder and chocolate chips with ½ cup plus 1 tablespoon carob powder and ½ cup vegan carob chips.

Per cookie: Calories 160, Protein 2 g, Fat 9 g, Carbohydrate 20 g, Fiber 2 g, Sodium 54 mg

Chocolate Walnut Brownie Cookies

☆ ☆

Makes 2 dozen cookies

The walnuts give this cookie a brownie-like texture, hence the name!

3/4 cup rolled oats

1/2 cup plus 2 tablespoons maple syrup

1/4 cup plus 2 tablespoons canola, safflower, or sunflower oil

1/2 teaspoon vanilla

3/4 cup chocolate chips

1 cup whole walnuts

1 cup barley flour

1/2 cup plus 1 tablespoon cocoa powder

1/2 cup Sucanat, date sugar, or maple sugar

1/2 teaspoon baking powder

1/2 teaspoon salt

Preheat the oven to 350°F. Process the oats in a food processor or blender until they are the consistency of coarse flour. In a small bowl, mix the syrup, oil, and vanilla; set aside.

In a separate, larger bowl, mix the ground oats, chocolate chips, and nuts. Sift the flour, cocoa, Sucanat, baking powder, and salt into the oat flour mixture. (Sifting isn't absolutely necessary, but it ensures there won't be clumps of flour or salt in the batter.) Pour the wet ingredients into the dry ingredients, and mix with a spatula until everything is well incorporated.

With a 1-ounce ice cream scoop or 2 spoons, scoop out 1 heaping tablespoon of the batter onto well-oiled or parchment-lined cookie sheets. Flatten the cookies slightly with the bottom of a cup or glass. (Dip the bottom of the cup or glass in warm water before flattening each cookie to prevent the batter from sticking to the glass.)

Bake for 11 minutes and rotate the cookie sheets a half turn to ensure even baking. Bake 5 minutes more or until the cookies are crisp around the edges. Let cool on the cookie sheets for 5 to 6 minutes before removing to a cooling rack.

For a chocolate mint cookie

Add 1 teaspoon of peppermint extract.

  Per cookie: Calories 159, Protein 2 g, Fat 9 g, Carbohydrate 20 g, Fiber 2 g, Sodium 36 mg

Chocolate Chip Cookies

☆ ☆

Makes 18 cookies

This is where it all began, with the quest for a vegan chocolate chip cookie. And here it is. No margarine, no tofu, no egg replacer—just vegan perfection. Experiment with this cookie. At Simple Treats Bakery, we have a favorite version called the Crazy Mixed-Up Nuts Cookie. We use roasted pecans, roasted almonds, walnuts, and macadamia nuts.

1 cup rolled oats

¼ cup plus 2 tablespoons canola, safflower, or sunflower oil

½ cup plus 2 tablespoons maple syrup

½ teaspoon vanilla

1 cup chocolate or vegan carob chips

¼ cup chopped nuts (optional)

1 cup barley flour

½ teaspoon baking soda

½ teaspoon baking powder

½ teaspoon salt

Preheat the oven to 350°F. Process the oats in a food processor or blender until they are the consistency of coarse flour. In a small bowl, mix the oil, syrup, and vanilla.

In a separate, larger bowl, place the ground oats, chocolate chips, and nuts, if using. Sift the flour, baking soda, baking powder, and salt into the oat mixture. (Sifting isn't absolutely necessary, but it ensures there won't be clumps of flour or salt in the batter.) Pour the wet ingredients into the dry ingredients and mix with a spatula until everything is well incorporated.

With a 1-ounce ice cream scoop or 2 spoons, scoop out 1 heaping tablespoon of the batter onto well-oiled or parchment-lined cookie sheets. Flatten the cookies slightly with the bottom of a cup or glass. (Dip the bottom of the cup or glass in warm water before flattening each cookie to prevent the batter from sticking to the glass.)

Bake for 11 minutes; rotate the cookie sheets a half turn to ensure even baking. Bake 5 to 6 minutes more or until the cookies are golden around the edges. Let cool on the cookie sheets for 5 to 6 minutes before removing to a cooling rack.

For a nuttier cookie

Add 1 cup roasted, skinned hazelnuts; process with rolled oats in the food processor or blender until they are the consistency of coarse flour.

Per cookie: Calories 159, Protein 2 g, Fat 8 g, Carbohydrate 21 g, Fiber 2 g, Sodium 106 mg

Chocolate Chip-Hemp Nut Seed Cookies

☆ ☆

Makes 18 cookies

This cookie is bold and political, and it's tasty enough to get away with it—yummy!!! Hemp seeds themselves contain 9% omega-3s and 31% high-quality complete protein. They're the "soybeans" of the next millennium, so enjoy, dude.

1 cup rolled oats

¼ cup plus 2 tablespoons canola, safflower, or sunflower oil

½ cup plus 2 tablespoons maple syrup

½ teaspoon vanilla

1 cup chocolate or vegan carob chips

1 cup roasted hemp nut seeds

¼ cup chopped nuts (optional)

1 cup barley flour

½ teaspoon baking soda

½ teaspoon baking powder

½ teaspoon salt

Preheat the oven to 350°F. Process the oats in a food processor or blender until they are the consistency of coarse flour. In a small bowl, mix the oil, syrup, and vanilla.

In a separate, larger bowl, place the ground oats, chocolate chips, hemp nut seeds, and nuts, if using. Sift the flour, baking soda, baking powder, and salt into the oat mixture. (Sifting isn't absolutely necessary, but it ensures there won't be clumps of flour or salt in the batter.) Pour the wet ingredients into the dry ingredients and mix with a spatula until everything is well incorporated.

With a 1-ounce ice cream scoop or 2 spoons, scoop out 1 heaping tablespoon of the batter onto well-oiled or parchment-lined cookie sheets. Flatten the cookies slightly with the bottom of a cup or glass. (Dip the bottom of the cup or glass in warm water before flattening each cookie to prevent the batter from sticking to the glass.)

Bake for 11 minutes; rotate the cookie sheets a half turn to ensure even baking. Bake 5 to 6 minutes more or until the cookies are golden around the edges. Let cool on the cookie sheets for 5 to 6 minutes before removing to a cooling rack.

For Crispy Rice Chocolate Chip Cookies

Omit hemp nut seeds. Add ¾ cup crisp rice cereal and increase nuts to 1 cup.

 Per cookie: Calories 159, Protein 3 g, Fat 8 g, Carbohydrate 21 g, Fiber 4 g, Sodium 106 mg

Chocolate Peanut Butter Fudge Cookies

☆ *Makes about 2 dozen cookies*

The combination of chocolate and peanut butter has always been a favorite, but I could never find anything vegan, especially in a cookie—until now. This cookie took some work perfecting, but peanut butter and chocolate have never tasted better. This cookie is truly a decadent favorite.

½ cup rolled oats

½ cup plus 1 tablespoon maple syrup

¼ cup plus 2 tablespoons canola, safflower, or sunflower oil

1 cup crunchy peanut butter

½ teaspoon vanilla

¾ cup chocolate chips *Tropical Source Brand*

⅓ cup barley flour

½ cup plus 1 tablespoon cocoa powder

½ cup Sucanat, date sugar, or maple sugar

½ teaspoon baking soda

½ teaspoon baking powder

½ teaspoon salt

Preheat the oven to 350°F. Process the oats in a food processor or blender until they are the consistency of coarse flour. In a small bowl, mix the syrup, oil, peanut butter, and vanilla.

In a separate, larger bowl, place the ground oats and the chocolate chips. Sift the flour, cocoa, Sucanat, baking soda, baking powder, and salt into the oat mixture. (Sifting isn't absolutely necessary, but it ensures there won't be clumps of flour or salt in the batter.) Pour the wet ingredients into the dry ingredients, and mix with a spatula until everything is well incorporated.

With a 1-ounce ice cream scoop or 2 spoons, scoop out 1 heaping tablespoon of the batter onto well-oiled or parchment-lined cookie sheets. Flatten the cookies slightly with the bottom of a cup or glass. (Dip the bottom of the cup or glass in warm water before flattening each cookie to prevent the batter from sticking to the glass.)

Bake for 10 minutes and rotate the cookie sheets a half turn to ensure even baking. Bake 5 minutes more or until the cookies are golden around the edges. Let cool on the cookie sheets for 5 to 6 minutes before removing to a cooling rack.

Per cookie: Calories 173, Protein 4 g, Fat 10 g, Carbohydrate 18 g, Fiber 2 g, Sodium 104 mg

Chocolate Chip Blondies

☆ *Makes six 2" to 3" squares*

These golden brownies don't last very long in the small natural food markets of New York City, especially in my sister Karen's neighborhood; she buys them out before the week is through. These are one of our best sellers and a personal favorite of mine.

1¼ cups rolled oats

¼ cup plus 2 tablespoons canola, safflower, or sunflower oil

¼ cup plus 2 tablespoons maple syrup

2 tablespoons brown rice syrup

1 teaspoon vanilla

½ cup chocolate chips or 1 cup vegan carob chips

⅓ cup chopped nuts (optional)

½ cup plus 1 tablespoon barley flour

½ teaspoon baking soda

½ teaspoon baking powder

½ teaspoon salt

Topping:

¼ cup chopped walnuts

Preheat the oven to 350°F. Oil an 8 x 8" baking pan. Process the oats in a food processor or blender until they are the consistency of coarse flour. In a small bowl, mix the oil, syrups, and vanilla; set aside.

In a separate, larger bowl, place the ground oats, chocolate chips, and chopped nuts, if using. Sift the flour, baking soda, baking powder, and salt into the oat mixture. (Sifting isn't absolutely necessary, but it ensures there won't be clumps of flour or salt in the batter.) Pour the wet ingredients into the dry ingredients, and mix with a spatula until everything is well incorporated.

Pour the batter into the prepared pan; sprinkle with the chopped walnuts.

Bake for 15 minutes and rotate the pan half a turn to ensure even baking. Bake 6 to 7 minutes more or until it is golden around the edges. Let cool for at least 30 minutes before cutting.

Per serving: Calories 405, Protein 6 g, Fat 22 g, Carbohydrate 47 g, Fiber 4 g, Sodium 316 mg

Brown Rice Krispy Treats

☆   Makes six 2½" squares

These are so delicious—a natural food version of a childhood favorite.

2½ tablespoons canola, safflower, or
   sunflower oil
½ cup brown rice syrup
2 tablespoons maple syrup
2 tablespoons barley malt syrup
½ teaspoon salt
6 cups brown rice cereal

Oil an 8 x 8" baking pan; set aside.

In a hot skillet over medium heat, heat the oil. Reduce the heat to low, and add the syrups and salt. Cook until the mixture begins to turn a deep golden brown. (This burns easily, so be sure to keep an eye on it.)

Pour the syrup mixture into a large, oiled bowl. Fold in the rice cereal until it is well coated with the syrup. Pour the mixture into the prepared pan. Cool 10 to 15 minutes before cutting.

To make these really special, top the cooled treats with melted chocolate.

Per serving: Calories 269, Protein 1 g, Fat 6 g, Carbohydrate 57 g, Fiber 1 g, Sodium 181 mg

Cakes

Basic Vanilla Cake

☆ ☆

Makes one 2-layer 8" cake
or one 9 x 13" cake

There is something so nice about the simplicity of this cake. At Simple Treats Bakery, we also use this cake as a base for several of our desserts. There are so many different cakes to create from this recipe: Add nuts, dried fruit, and fresh fruit—use your imagination.

¼ cup canola, safflower, or sunflower oil

¼ cup maple syrup

2 cups soymilk

2 teaspoons apple cider vinegar

2 teaspoons vanilla

½ cup maple sugar, Sucanat, or date sugar

3½ cups barley flour

2 teaspoons baking soda

2 teaspoons baking powder

¼ teaspoon grated nutmeg

1 teaspoon salt

Preheat the oven to 350°F. Oil two 8" round cake pans or one 9 x 13" cake pan, and set aside.

Mix the oil, syrup, soymilk, vinegar, and vanilla in a small bowl.

In a separate, larger bowl, place the sugar and sift the flour, baking soda, baking powder, nutmeg, and salt into the sugar. (Sifting isn't absolutely necessary, but it ensures there won't be clumps of flour or salt in the batter.)

Whisk the wet ingredients into the dry ingredients until well incorporated; finish mixing with a spatula to scrape the sides of the bowl. Pour the batter into the prepared pans.

Bake for 25 minutes and rotate the pans a half turn to ensure even baking. Bake 5 to 6 minutes more or until a knife inserted in the center comes out clean. Let cool for about 10 minutes; remove from the pans and let cool completely on a wire rack.

For Chocolate Chip Cake

Add 1 cup chocolate chips.

For Berry Cake

Add 1 cup chopped strawberries or other berries.

For Vanilla Spice Cake

Add ¼ teaspoon ground cinnamon and ¼ teaspoon ground allspice.

For cupcakes, pour the batter into an oiled muffin pan. Bake at 350°F for 20 to 25 minutes or until the cupcakes spring back when pressed lightly with your finger. Makes 12 cupcakes.

 Per serving (serves 12): Calories 220, Protein 5 g, Fat 6 g, Carbohydrate 39 g, Fiber 6 g, Sodium 454 mg

Raspberry-Filled Vanilla Cake

Makes one 2-layer 8" cake

☆ ☆

1 Basic Vanilla Cake (page 74), baked in two 8" cake pans

¼ cup raspberry jam or fruit spread

1 pint fresh or frozen raspberries (if using frozen, do not thaw)

1 recipe Chocolate Tofu Crème Frosting (page 111)

Place 1 cake layer on a serving plate. Spread the top with raspberry jam or fruit spread. Gently press fresh raspberries evenly into jam.

Place the second cake layer on top. Gently press it to secure it in place.

Frost the entire cake with Chocolate Tofu Crème Frosting.

Per serving (serves 12): Calories 440, Protein 13 g, Fat 18 g, Carbohydrate 61 g, Fiber 81 g, Sodium 482 g

The Chocolate Crèmesicle

Makes one 2-layer 8" cake or one 9 x 13" cake

☆ ☆

This cake has a wonderful mélange of flavors: the sweetness of the orange, the subtle nuttiness of almonds, and the warming spices of our Vanilla Spice Cake— it is truly a very special treat.

1 Vanilla Spice Cake (page 74), baked in two 8" round pans or in one 9 x 13" pan

Brandy or Grand Marnier (optional)

1 cup Orange-Almond Crème (page 103)

1 recipe Chocolate Ganache (page 112)

If you are making a 9 x 13" cake, slice the cake in half horizontally with a large, serrated knife.

To assemble the cake, place 1 layer on a wire cooling rack placed over a sheet of foil or waxed paper to catch the drips. Sprinkle the layer with some brandy or Grand Marnier, if desired. Spread the Orange-Almond Crème on the cake to about ¼ inch from the edge.

Place the second cake layer on top of the filling. Gently press it to secure it in place. Pour the Chocolate Ganache over the entire cake, letting it drizzle evenly down the sides to cover the cake.

Per serving (serves 12): Calories 430, Protein 8 g, Fat 17 g, Carbohydrate 65 g, Fiber 7 g, Sodium 502 mg

Strawberry Shortcake

☆ Makes one 2-layer 8" cake or one 9 x 13" cake

This is a really nice way to enjoy fresh strawberries at their best, in the summertime when they are in season. If you love this recipe, and it happens to be the middle of winter, frozen berries will do nicely. This is beautiful in a large glass bowl and spooned out to serve. Any large, deep-sided dish will do.

1 Vanilla Spice Cake (page 74), baked in two 8" round pans or in one 9 x 13" pan

1 quart fresh strawberries
1 tablespoon maple sugar, Sucanat, or date sugar

Strawberry Sauce:

1½ cups fresh or frozen strawberries, thawed
3 tablespoons maple syrup
3 tablespoons soymilk
1 teaspoon vanilla
Pinch of salt

Grand Marnier or cognac (optional)
1 cup Cashew Crème (page 106)
Fresh mint and whole strawberries for garnish (optional)

Clean and slice the fresh strawberries into a bowl. Spoon the maple sugar over them, and let them sit, unrefrigerated, until ready to use.

To make Strawberry Sauce, process all of the sauce ingredients in a food processor. For a more refined sauce, pass the sauce through a sieve to remove the seeds. Set aside.

To assemble the shortcake, slice the cake layers in half horizontally. If making a 9 x 13" cake, cut the cake in half horizontally and then in pieces to fit your serving dishes or plates.

Place one cake layer on a serving plate or dish; sprinkle with Grand Marnier or cognac, if desired. Spoon some Strawberry Sauce over this cake layer, followed by some Cashew Crème and a layer of sliced strawberries. Top with the second layer of cake, more Strawberry Sauce, more Cashew Crème, and more sliced strawberries. Garnish with mint and whole strawberries, if desired. Serve with the remaining Strawberry Sauce on the side.

 Per serving (serves 12): Calories 366, Protein 8 g, Fat 13 g, Carbohydrate 58 g, Fiber 9 g, Sodium 480 mg

Basic Carob or Chocolate Cake

Makes one 2-layer 8" cake or
one 9 x 13" cake

☆ ☆

There is nothing "basic" about the flavor of this cake. It is rich and divine. There are so many different cakes to create starting from this recipe. For example, fill and frost with Chocolate or Carob Tofu Crème Frosting (page 111). Look through the recipes for other frostings, glazes, fillings, and toppings to make your own Simple Treat.

½ cup canola, safflower, or sunflower oil

½ cup maple syrup

2 cups plus 1 teaspoon soymilk

2 teaspoons apple cider vinegar

1 teaspoon vanilla

1 cup maple sugar, Sucanat, or date sugar

3 cups barley flour

½ cup plus 2 tablespoons cocoa or carob powder

2 teaspoons baking soda

2 teaspoons baking powder

½ teaspoon ground cinnamon

1 teaspoon salt

Preheat the oven to 350°F. Oil two 8" round cake pans or one 9 x 13" cake pan, and set aside. Mix the oil, syrup, soymilk, vinegar, and vanilla in a small bowl.

In a separate, larger bowl, place the sugar and sift the flour, cocoa, baking soda, baking powder, cinnamon, and salt into the sugar. (Sifting isn't absolutely necessary, but it ensures there won't be clumps of flour or salt in the batter.)

Whisk the wet ingredients into the dry ingredients until well incorporated. Finish mixing with a spatula to scrape the sides of the bowl. Pour the batter into the prepared pans.

Bake for 30 minutes and rotate the pans a half turn to ensure even baking. Bake 5 to 6 minutes more or until a knife inserted in the center comes out clean. Let cool for about 10 minutes; remove from the pans and let cool completely on a wire rack.

For super chocolate flavor, add 1 cup chocolate or carob chips to the batter.

For a fruity version, add 1 cup chopped cherries or berries to the batter.

For cupcakes, pour the batter into an oiled muffin pan. Bake at 350°F for 20 to 25 minutes or until the cupcakes spring back when pressed lightly with your finger. Makes 12 cupcakes.

Per serving (serves 12): Calories 302, Protein 5 g, Fat 11 g, Carbohydrate 50 g, Fiber 7 g, Sodium 456 mg

Marble Pound Cake

☆ *Makes one 8 x 4 x 2½" loaf*

This cake is traditionally loaded with butter—a pound, to be exact. We have removed all of the butter and replaced it with oil, using only a fraction of the original amount. It is a hearty cake that everyone is sure to love.

Vanilla batter:

3 tablespoons canola, safflower, or sunflower oil

2 tablespoons maple syrup

¼ cup soymilk

½ teaspoon apple cider vinegar

1 teaspoon vanilla

¾ cup barley flour

2 tablespoons maple sugar, Sucanat, or date sugar

½ teaspoon baking soda

½ teaspoon baking powder

⅛ teaspoon grated nutmeg

¼ teaspoon salt

Preheat the oven to 350°F. Oil a 8 x 4 x 2½" loaf pan; set aside.

To make the vanilla batter: In a small bowl, mix the oil, syrup, soymilk, vinegar, and vanilla. In a separate, larger bowl, sift the flour, sugar, baking soda, baking powder, nutmeg, and salt. (Sifting isn't absolutely necessary, but it ensures there won't be clumps of flour or salt in the batter.) Pour the wet ingredients into the dry ingredients, and mix well; set aside while preparing the chocolate batter.

☆ ☆

Chocolate batter:

3 tablespoons canola, safflower, or sunflower oil

2 tablespoons maple syrup

1/4 cup soymilk

1/2 teaspoon apple cider vinegar

1 teaspoon vanilla

3/4 cup barley flour

2 tablespoons plus 1/2 teaspoon cocoa powder

1/4 cup maple sugar, Sucanat, or date sugar

1/2 teaspoon baking soda

1/2 teaspoon baking powder

1/8 teaspoon ground cinnamon

1/4 teaspoon salt

To make the chocolate batter: In a small bowl, mix the oil, syrup, soymilk, vinegar, and vanilla. In a separate, larger bowl, sift the flour, cocoa, sugar, baking soda, baking powder, cinnamon, and salt. (Sifting isn't absolutely necessary, but it ensures there won't be clumps of flour or salt in the batter.) Pour the wet ingredients into the dry ingredients, and mix well.

To assemble, pour 1/2 of the vanilla batter into the prepared pan. Pour 1/2 of the chocolate batter over the vanilla batter in the pan. Pour the remaining vanilla batter over the chocolate batter; pour the remaining chocolate batter over the vanilla batter. With a knife, cut through the batters just enough to create several swirls.

Bake for 35 minutes and rotate the pan a half turn to ensure even baking. Bake 30 minutes more or until a knife inserted in the center comes out clean. Let cool for about 15 minutes; remove from the pan and let cool completely on a wire rack before slicing.

This cake is very rich and doesn't need a frosting—just a dusting of sifted maple sugar.

For super chocolate flavor, add 3/4 cup chocolate chips.

You can also make this an all-vanilla or an all-chocolate pound cake by doubling either batter recipe.

Per serving (serves 12): Calories 160, Protein 2 g, Fat 8 g, Carbohydrate 23 g, Fiber 3 g, Sodium 226 mg

Chocolate Coconut Cake

☆☆☆☆☆☆☆☆☆☆☆☆☆☆☆☆☆☆☆☆☆☆☆☆☆☆ **Makes one 2-layer 8" cake**

This cake is wonderfully rich and moist.

½ cup canola, safflower, or sunflower oil

½ cup maple syrup

2 cups soymilk

2 teaspoons apple cider vinegar

1 teaspoon vanilla

1 teaspoon coconut extract

1 cup maple sugar or Sucanat

1 cup toasted, shredded coconut

3 cups barley flour

½ cup plus 2 tablespoons cocoa powder

2 teaspoons baking soda

2 teaspoons baking powder

¼ teaspoon ground cinnamon

1 teaspoon salt

For cupcakes, pour the batter into an oiled muffin pan. Bake at 350°F for 20 to 25 minutes or until the cupcakes spring back when pressed lightly with your finger. Makes 12 cupcakes.

Preheat the oven to 350°F. Oil two 8" round cake pans, and set aside.

Mix the oil, syrup, soymilk, vinegar, vanilla, and coconut extract in a small bowl. In a separate, larger bowl, place the sugar and the coconut, and sift the flour, cocoa, baking soda, baking powder, cinnamon, and salt into the sugar-coconut mixture. (Sifting isn't absolutely necessary, but it ensures there won't be clumps of flour or salt in the batter.)

Whisk the wet ingredients into the dry ingredients until well incorporated. Do not overwork the batter. Finish mixing with a spatula to scrape the sides of the bowl. Pour the batter into the prepared pans.

Bake for 30 minutes and rotate the pans a half turn to ensure even baking. Bake 5 to 6 minutes more or until a knife inserted in the center comes out clean. Let cool for about 10 minutes; remove from the pans and let cool completely on a wire rack.

Serving suggestion: Fill and frost the cake with Chocolate Tofu Crème Frosting (page 111) and sprinkle the top and sides with toasted coconut.

For Chocolate Chip Coconut Cake

Add 1 cup chocolate chips.

For Berry Coconut Cake

Add 1¼ cups chopped strawberries or other berries.

Per serving (serves 12): Calories 427, Protein 7 g, Fat 23 g, Carbohydrate 55 g, Fiber 10 g, Sodium 463 mg

Peanut Butter Cake

☆ ☆

This cake was inspired by my love for peanut butter. I mean, if we can make cookies and sandwiches with it, why not cake? Pair it with our Chocolate Tofu Crème Frosting, and this is truly a fabulous dessert.

1 cup peanut butter

¼ cup canola, safflower, or sunflower oil

¼ cup maple syrup

2 cups soymilk

2 teaspoons apple cider vinegar

2 tablespoons vanilla

½ cup maple sugar, Sucanat, or date sugar

3½ cups barley flour

2 teaspoons baking soda

2 teaspoons baking powder

1 teaspoon salt

1 recipe Chocolate Tofu Crème Frosting (page 111)

For cupcakes, pour the batter into an oiled muffin pan. Bake at 350°F for 20 to 25 minutes or until the cupcakes spring back when pressed lightly with your finger. Makes 12 cupcakes.

Preheat the oven to 350° F. Oil two 8" cake pans or one 9 x 13" cake pan and set aside.

Mix the peanut butter, oil, syrup, soymilk, vinegar, and vanilla in a medium bowl.

In a separate, larger bowl, place the sugar; sift the flour, baking soda, baking powder, and salt into the sugar. (Sifting isn't absolutely necessary, but it ensures there won't be clumps of flour or salt in the batter.) Whisk the wet ingredients into the dry ingredients until well incorporated. Finish mixing with a spatula to scrape the sides of the bowl. Pour the batter into the prepared pans.

Bake for 25 minutes and rotate the pans a half turn to ensure even baking. Bake 5 to 6 minutes more or until a knife inserted in the center comes out clean. Let cool for about 10 minutes; remove from pans and let cool completely on a wire rack. Frost with Chocolate Tofu Crème Frosting.

For a Chocolate Chip Peanut Butter Cake

Add 1 cup chocolate chips.

For a nuttier cake

Add 1 cup chopped, roasted peanuts (page 101).

For Chocolate Frosted Peanut Butter Cake

Fill and frost with Chocolate Tofu Crème Frosting (page 111). Sprinkle the filling with roasted, chopped peanuts.

 Per serving (serves 12): Calories 373, Protein 12 g, Fat 16 g, Carbohydrate 54 g, Fiber 8 g, Sodium 507 mg

Chocolate Peanut Butter Cake

☆ ☆

Makes one 2-layer 8" cake or one 9 x 13" cake

This cake is simply divine. It is very rich and delicious, so make sure you share it with friends and family. Otherwise, you may end up eating it all on your own!

1 cup peanut butter

¼ cup canola, safflower, or sunflower oil

¼ cup maple syrup

2 cups soymilk

2 teaspoons apple cider vinegar

2 teaspoons vanilla

1 cup maple sugar, Sucanat, or date sugar

3 cups barley flour

½ cup plus 2 tablespoons cocoa powder

2 teaspoons baking soda

2 teaspoons baking powder

1 teaspoon salt

For cupcakes, pour the batter into an oiled muffin pan. Bake at 350°F for 20 to 25 minutes or until the cupcakes spring back when pressed lightly with your finger. Makes 12 cupcakes.

Preheat the oven to 350°F. Oil two 8" round cake pans or one 9 x 13" cake pan, and set aside. Mix the peanut butter, oil, syrup, soymilk, vinegar, and vanilla in a medium bowl.

In a separate, larger bowl, place the sugar and sift the flour, cocoa, baking soda, baking powder, and salt into the sugar. (Sifting isn't absolutely necessary, but it ensures there won't be clumps of flour or salt in the batter.)

Whisk the wet ingredients into the dry ingredients until well incorporated. Finish mixing with a spatula to scrape the sides of the bowl. Pour the batter into the prepared pans.

Bake for 25 minutes and rotate the pans a half turn to ensure even baking. Bake 5 to 6 minutes more or until a knife inserted in the center comes out clean. Let cool for about 10 minutes; remove from pans and let cool completely on a wire rack.

For super chocolate flavor, add 1 cup chocolate chips.

For a nuttier version, add 1 cup chopped, roasted peanuts (page 101).

For Double Chocolate Peanut Butter Cake

Fill and frost with Chocolate Tofu Crème Frosting (page 111). Sprinkle the filling with roasted, chopped peanuts.

Per serving (serves 12): Calories 373, Protein 11 g, Fat 16 g, Carbohydrate 51 g, Fiber 8 g, Sodium 505 mg

Mocha Cake

☆ ☆

You would never suspect that it isn't real coffee that gives this cake its flavor. It's sure to satisfy even the most sophisticated coffee lover.

½ cup canola, safflower, or sunflower oil

½ cup maple syrup

2 cups plus 2 tablespoons soymilk

2 teaspoons apple cider vinegar

1 tablespoon coffee extract

1 tablespoon vanilla

1 cup maple sugar, Sucanat, or date sugar

1 cup coffee substitute powder or granules

3 cups barley flour

½ cup plus 2 tablespoons cocoa powder

2 teaspoons baking soda

2 teaspoons baking powder

1 teaspoon salt

Preheat the oven to 350°F. Oil two 8" round cake pans or one 9 x 13" cake pan, and set aside.

Mix the oil, syrup, soymilk, vinegar, coffee extract, and vanilla in a small bowl.

In a separate, larger bowl, mix the sugar and coffee substitute, and sift the flour, cocoa, baking soda, baking powder, and salt into the coffee mixture. (Sifting isn't absolutely necessary, but it ensures there won't be clumps of flour or salt in the batter.)

Whisk the wet ingredients into the dry ingredients until well incorporated. Finish mixing with a spatula to scrape the sides of the bowl. Pour the batter into the prepared pans.

Bake for 25 minutes and rotate the pans a half turn to ensure even baking. Bake 10 minutes more or until a knife inserted in the center comes out clean. Let cool for about 15 minutes; remove from the pans and let cool completely on a wire rack.

For a rich dessert, fill and frost cake with Mocha Crème (page 103). It is equally wonderful frosted with the Chocolate Ganache (page 112) or Chocolate Tofu Crème Frosting (page 111).

For super chocolate flavor, add ¾ cup chocolate chips.

For cupcakes, pour the batter into an oiled muffin pan. Bake at 350°F for 20 to 25 minutes or until the cupcakes spring back when pressed lightly with your finger. Makes 12 cupcakes.

★ Per serving (serves 12): Calories 328, Protein 6 g, Fat 11 g, Carbohydrate 54 g, Fiber 7 g, Sodium 456 mg ★

Lemon Cake

☆ ☆

Makes one 2-layer 8" cake or one 9 x 13" cake

This is a nice cake for brunches and afternoon celebrations.

½ cup canola, safflower, or sunflower oil

½ cup maple syrup

1 cup soymilk

Juice and zest of 2 lemons (about ½ cup juice, 3 tablespoons zest)

1 teaspoon vanilla

2 teaspoons lemon extract

½ cup maple sugar, Sucanat, or date sugar

4 cups barley flour

2 teaspoons baking soda

2 teaspoons baking powder

1 teaspoon salt

Poppy seeds and extra maple sugar

Preheat the oven to 350°F. Oil two 8" round cake pans or one 9 x 13" cake pan, and set aside.

Mix the oil, syrup, soymilk, juice, zest, vanilla, and lemon extract in a medium bowl.

In a separate, larger bowl, place the sugar; sift the flour, baking soda, baking powder, and salt into the sugar. (Sifting isn't absolutely necessary, but it ensures there won't be clumps of flour or salt in the batter.)

Whisk the wet ingredients into the dry ingredients until well incorporated. Do not overwork the batter. If the batter seems stiff, add 1 to 2 teaspoons soymilk. Finish mixing with a spatula to scrape the sides of the bowl. Pour the batter into the prepared pans. Sprinkle with poppy seeds and sugar.

Bake for 30 minutes and rotate the pans a half turn to ensure even baking. Bake 20 to 25 minutes more or until a knife inserted in the center comes out clean. Let cool for about 15 minutes; remove from the pans and let cool completely on a wire rack.

Per serving (serves 12): Calories 258, Protein 5 g, Fat 10 g, Carbohydrate 39 g, Fiber 7 g, Sodium 452 mg

Raspberry-Filled Lemon Cake

☆ **Makes one 2-layer 8" cake**

I have always loved the combination of raspberries and lemon. It is so refreshing and balanced with just enough tartness to bring out the sweet. This is one of my favorite cakes.

1 Lemon Cake (previous page), baked in two 8" cake pans

½ cup raspberry jam

¾ cup fresh or frozen raspberries, slightly crushed

1 recipe Lemon Glaze (page 113)

Maple powder

1 recipe Almond Crème (page 102)

More fresh or frozen, slightly crushed raspberries to serve on the side (if frozen, do not thaw)

Mint leaves and edible flowers for garnish (optional)

Place one cake layer on a serving plate; spread the top with the raspberry jam to the edges of the cake. Top with ¾ cup of the raspberries.

Place the second cake layer on top of the raspberries and raspberry filling. Gently press it to secure it in place. Drizzle the Lemon Glaze over the top of the cake, and dust the top with maple powder.

Serve with Almond Crème and a spoonful of crushed raspberries. Garnish with mint leaves and edible flowers, if desired.

Per serving (serves 12): Calories 484, Protein 8 g, Fat 17 g, Carbohydrate 56 g, Fiber 9 g, Sodium 477 mg

Orange Cake

☆ **Makes one 2-layer 8" cake or one 9 x 13" cake**

This elegant cake is so easy to prepare.

½ cup canola, safflower, or sunflower oil

½ cup maple syrup

Juice and zest of 2 oranges (about 1 cup juice, 4 tablespoons zest)

¾ cup soymilk

¼ teaspoon apple cider vinegar

1 tablespoon Grand Marnier or Cointreau (optional)

2 teaspoons vanilla

½ cup maple sugar, Sucanat, or date sugar

3½ cups barley flour

2 teaspoons baking soda

2 teaspoons baking powder

1 teaspoon salt

Preheat the oven to 350°F. Oil two 8" round cake pans or one 9 x 13" cake pan and set aside.

Mix the oil, syrup, juice, zest, soymilk, vinegar, Grand Marnier (if desired), and vanilla in a small bowl.

In a separate, larger bowl, place the sugar and sift the flour, baking soda, baking powder, and salt into the sugar. (Sifting isn't absolutely necessary, but it ensures there won't be clumps of flour or salt in the batter.)

Whisk the wet ingredients into the dry ingredients until well incorporated. Finish mixing with a spatula to scrape the sides of the bowl. Pour the batter into the prepared pans.

Bake for 25 minutes and rotate the pans a half turn to ensure even baking. Bake 5 to 6 minutes more or until a knife inserted in the center comes out clean. Let cool for about 10 minutes; remove from the pans and cool completely on a wire rack.

⭐ Per serving (serves 12): Calories 280, Protein 5 g, Fat 10 g, Carbohydrate 45 g, Fiber 6 g, Sodium 452 mg ⭐

Cake L'Orange

☆ ☆ ☆ ☆ ☆ ☆ ☆ ☆ ☆ ☆ ☆ ☆ ☆ ☆ ☆ ☆ ☆ ☆ ☆

Makes one 2-layer 8" cake

This is a spectacular dessert, absolutely filled with flavor and sure to please just about anyone with a sweet tooth. If you love the flavors of orange and chocolate together, this cake is for you.

1 Orange Cake (previous page), baked in two 8" cake pans

4 tablespoons orange liqueur, such as Grand Marnier or Cointreau, divided

¼ cup orange marmalade

1 recipe Chocolate Tofu Crème Frosting (page 111)

Fresh mint sprigs and orange slices for garnish

Place 1 cake layer on a serving plate; sprinkle it with 2 tablespoons liqueur. Spread the top with the orange marmalade.

On the bottom side of the second layer, sprinkle the remaining liqueur. Place it liqueur-side down on top of the first layer. Gently press it to secure it in place.

Frost the entire cake with Chocolate Tofu Crème Frosting. Garnish with mint and orange slices.

 Per serving (serves 12): Calories 335, Protein 5 g, Fat 11 g, Carbohydrate 54 g, Fiber 6 g, Sodium 458 mg

Baked Apple-Cranberry Crisp

☆☆☆☆☆☆☆☆☆☆☆☆☆☆☆☆☆☆☆☆☆

Makes 6 to 8 servings

This simple dessert is warming and delicious—and an amazing way to use up fruit that might be a little past its prime. Everyone always thinks you've worked so hard on this dessert when you present them with this scrumptious, bubbling confection. It's delicious fresh out of the oven with a scoop of vegan vanilla "ice cream."

Topping:

¼ cup barley flour

½ cup maple sugar, Sucanat, or date sugar

2 tablespoons ground cinnamon

¼ teaspoon salt

¼ cup walnuts

¾ cup rolled oats

3 tablespoons canola, safflower, or sunflower oil

Filling:

4 cups sliced, peeled apples (about 5 apples)

1 cup fresh cranberries

2 tablespoons lemon juice

¼ cup maple sugar, Sucanat, or date sugar

1 tablespoon ground cinnamon

Dash each of grated nutmeg, ground allspice, and salt

Dash of cayenne pepper (optional)

2 tablespoons arrowroot

Preheat the oven to 400°F. Oil a 2-quart baking dish or casserole, and set aside.

To make the topping, sift the flour, sugar, cinnamon, and salt into a small bowl; add the walnuts and oats. Mix with a knife or a fork to combine the ingredients well. Drizzle in the oil while stirring with a knife; stir until all of the oil is mixed in and the mixture resembles coarse crumbs.

To make the filling, combine the apples, cranberries, juice, sugar, spices, and arrowroot, and toss until everything is well coated. Spread the apple mixture in the prepared dish, and cover with the topping.

Bake for 10 minutes, then reduce the heat to 350°F. Bake 25 minutes more until the topping is browned, the filling is bubbly, and the apples are soft.

For a change of taste, try substituting raisins for the cranberries, and/or pears for the apples.

Per serving: Calories 282, Protein 3 g, Fat 10 g, Carbohydrate 53 g, Fiber 5 g, Sodium 77 mg

The Perfect Crumb Cake

☆ ☆

Makes one 9 x 13" cake

We would call this the perfect coffee cake, but Jill and I have given up coffee for something not so caffeinated. This cake is so wonderful and the smell that fills the house is reason enough to make it. The crumb topping is totally personal—nuts, no nuts, raisins—be creative.

Crumb Topping:

- ½ cup plus 2 tablespoons barley flour
- ½ cup plus 1 tablespoon maple sugar, Sucanat, or date sugar
- 2 teaspoons ground cinnamon
- ½ teaspoon salt
- ½ cup chopped walnuts
- ¼ cup plus 2 tablespoons canola, safflower, or sunflower oil

Batter:

- ½ cup canola, safflower, or sunflower oil
- ½ cup maple syrup
- 2 cups soymilk
- 2 teaspoons apple cider vinegar
- 1 tablespoon vanilla
- ½ cup maple sugar, Sucanat, or date sugar
- 3½ cups barley flour
- 2 teaspoons baking soda
- 2 teaspoons baking powder
- 2 tablespoons ground cinnamon
- 1 teaspoon salt

Preheat the oven to 350° F. Oil a 9 x 13" cake pan, and set aside.

To make the Crumb Topping: Sift the flour, sugar, cinnamon, and salt into a small bowl; add the walnuts. Mix with a knife or a fork to combine the ingredients well. Drizzle in the oil while stirring with a knife; stir until all of the oil is mixed in and the mixture resembles coarse crumbs; set aside.

To make the Batter: Mix the oil, syrup, soymilk, vinegar, and vanilla in a small bowl. In a separate, larger bowl, place the sugar and sift all of the remaining ingredients into the sugar. (Sifting isn't absolutely necessary, but it ensures there won't be clumps of flour or salt in the batter.)

Whisk the wet ingredients into the dry ingredients until well incorporated. Do not overwork the batter. Finish mixing with a spatula to scrape the sides of the bowl. Pour the batter into the prepared pan. Sprinkle the batter with the crumb topping.

Bake for 35 minutes and rotate the pan a half turn to ensure even baking. Bake 35 to 40 minutes more or until a knife inserted in the center comes out clean. Let cool for 15 to 20 minutes before slicing.

For Blueberry Crumb Cake

Add 1 cup fresh or frozen blueberries to the Crumb Topping.

For Pineapple Crumb Cake

Add 1 cup chopped fresh or canned pineapple to the Crumb Topping.

 Per serving (serves 12): Calories 427, Protein 7 g, Fat 21 g, Carbohydrate 57 g, Fiber 7 g, Sodium 544 mg

Decadent Carob or Chocolate Mousse Cake

☆   **Makes one 2-layer 8" cake**

This was one of the first rich desserts we devised for our bakery. It is also one of the best. The mousse is an unbelievable accompaniment to the chocolate cake. This is our favorite birthday cake. Making the mousse ahead of time makes putting this piece of work together a breeze. Everyone has a happy day when they have a slice of this intoxicating dessert.

1 Basic Carob or Chocolate Cake (page 77), baked in two 8" round pans

Brandy or flavored liqueur, such as Frangelico (optional)

1 cup Chocolate Mousse (page 104)

1 recipe Chocolate Tofu Crème Frosting (page 111)

Place 1 cake layer on a serving plate. Sprinkle it with some brandy, if desired. Spread Chocolate Mousse on the top of the layer to about ¼ inch from the edge.

Place the second cake layer on top of the filling. Gently press it to secure it in place. Frost the entire cake with the Chocolate Tofu Crème Frosting.

Per serving (serves 12): Calories 649, Protein 15 g, Fat 31 g, Carbohydrate 85 g, Fiber 9 g, Sodium 529 mg

Chocolate Chip Black Cherry Cake

☆ ☆

This cake is simple but delicious and very easy to put together. What a wonderful way to celebrate the day, by making this quick and easy sweet treat.

1 Basic Chocolate Cake (page 77), baked in two 8" round pans

³/₄ cup chocolate chips

¼ cup black cherry preserves, jam, or fruit spread

1 cup fresh or frozen cherries, roughly chopped

1 recipe Chocolate Ganache (page 112)

Just before baking, sprinkle the batter in each pan with 6 tablespoons chocolate chips.

Place one cake layer, chip-side up, on a wire rack placed over a sheet of foil or waxed paper to catch the drips. Spread the preserves on top of the first layer. Gently press the chopped cherries evenly into the jam.

Place the second cake layer, chip-side down, on top of the cherries.

Gently press it to secure it in place. Frost the entire cake with Chocolate Ganache.

 Per serving (serves 12): Calories 552, Protein 8 g, Fat 23 g, Carbohydrate 85 g, Fiber 8 g, Sodium 504 mg

Chocolate Raspberry Cake with Chocolate Ganache

☆ ☆

Makes one 8" cake or bundt cake

Berries and chocolate are a fantastic combination for any occasion. The berries make this cake a truly special indulgence.

¼ cup canola, safflower, or sunflower oil

¼ cup maple syrup

1 cup soymilk

1 teaspoon apple cider vinegar

1 teaspoon raspberry extract

1 teaspoon vanilla

¼ cup maple sugar, Sucanat, or date sugar

1½ cups barley flour

¼ cup plus 1 tablespoon cocoa powder

1 teaspoon baking soda

1 teaspoon baking powder

½ teaspoon salt

¾ cup fresh or frozen raspberries, roughly chopped (if frozen, do not thaw)

1 recipe Chocolate Ganache (page 112)

Fresh mint sprigs and fresh raspberries for garnish

Preheat the oven to 350°F. Oil an 8" round or square pan or bundt pan and set aside.

Mix the oil, syrup, soymilk, vinegar, raspberry extract, and vanilla in a small bowl.

In a separate, larger bowl, place the sugar and sift the flour, cocoa, baking soda, baking powder, and salt into the sugar. (Sifting isn't absolutely necessary, but it ensures there won't be clumps of flour or salt in the batter.) Whisk the wet ingredients into the dry ingredients until well incorporated. Do not overwork the batter. Finish mixing with a spatula to scrape the sides of the bowl. Fold in the raspberries. Pour the batter into the prepared pan.

Bake for 30 minutes and rotate the pans a half turn to ensure even baking. Bake 5 minutes more or until a knife inserted in the center comes out clean. Let cool for about 10 minutes; remove from the pan and cool completely on a wire rack.

Place the cake on a wire rack over a sheet of foil or waxed paper to catch the drips. Pour the Chocolate Ganache evenly over the cake. Garnish with mint sprigs and fresh raspberries.

 Per serving (serves 12): Calories 310, Protein 4 g, Fat 14 g, Carbohydrate 44 g, Fiber 4 g, Sodium 274 mg

Almond Ring Cake with Raspberry Maple Glaze

☆ *Makes one 8" round or square cake or bundt cake*

This cake is wonderful. Almonds and raspberries are one of my favorite combinations.

½ cup roasted almonds (page 101)

1¾ cups barley flour, divided

¼ cup canola, safflower, or sunflower oil

¼ cup maple syrup

1 cup soymilk

2 teaspoons apple cider vinegar

1 teaspoon almond extract

1 teaspoon vanilla

¼ cup maple sugar, Sucanat, or date sugar

1 teaspoon baking soda

1 teaspoon baking powder

¼ teaspoon ground cinnamon

½ teaspoon salt

1 recipe Raspberry Maple Glaze (page 110)

Preheat the oven to 350° F. Oil an 8" round or square pan or a bundt pan and set aside.

Process the cooled, roasted almonds and 1 cup of the flour in a food processor or blender until they are the consistency of fine meal.

Mix the oil, syrup, soymilk, vinegar, almond extract, and vanilla in a small bowl. In a separate, larger bowl, place the sugar and almond-flour mixture, and sift the remaining flour, baking soda, baking powder, cinnamon, and salt into the sugar mixture. (Sifting isn't absolutely necessary, but it ensures there won't be clumps of flour or salt in the batter.)

Whisk the wet ingredients into the dry ingredients until well incorporated. Do not overwork the batter. Finish mixing with a spatula to scrape the sides of the bowl. Pour the batter into the prepared pan.

Bake for 25 minutes and rotate the pan a half turn to ensure even baking. Bake 5 to 6 minutes more or until a knife inserted in the center comes out clean. Let cool for about 10 minutes; remove from the pan and cool completely on a wire rack. Frost with Raspberry Maple Glaze.

 Per serving (serves 12): Calories 332, Protein 4 g, Fat 9 g, Carbohydrate 64 g, Fiber 4 g, Sodium 278 mg

Carrot Cake with Cashew Crème and Maple Walnut Glaze

☆ ☆

Makes one 2-layer 8" cake or one 9 x 13" cake

This moist little cake is filled with nuts, raisins, and wonderful spices.

½ cup canola, safflower, or sunflower oil

½ cup maple syrup

¼ cup barley malt syrup

1¼ cups soymilk

2 teaspoons apple cider vinegar

2 teaspoons vanilla

½ cup chopped walnuts (optional)

½ cup golden raisins (optional)

¼ cup plus 2 tablespoons maple sugar, Sucanat, or date sugar

3½ cups barley flour

2 teaspoons baking soda

2 teaspoons baking powder

2 teaspoons ground cinnamon

1 teaspoon powdered ginger

1 teaspoon ground cloves

1 teaspoon ground allspice

½ teaspoon grated nutmeg

1 teaspoon salt

3½ cups shredded carrots, not packed

Brandy (optional)

½ cup Cashew Crème (page 106)

1 recipe Maple Walnut Glaze (page 110)

Preheat the oven to 350°F. Oil two 8" round cake pans or one 9 x 13" cake pan, and set aside.

Mix the oil, syrups, soymilk, vinegar, and vanilla in a small bowl.

In a separate, larger bowl, place the walnuts, raisins (if desired), and sugar. Sift the flour, baking soda, baking powder, spices, and salt into the walnut mixture. (Sifting isn't absolutely necessary, but it ensures there won't be clumps of flour or salt in the batter.) Whisk the wet ingredients into the dry ingredients until well incorporated. If the batter seems very stiff, add 1 teaspoon of soymilk. Do not overwork the batter.

Fold in the carrots. Pour the batter into the prepared pans.

Bake for 30 minutes and rotate the pans a half turn to ensure even baking. Bake 6 to 7 minutes more or until a knife inserted in the center comes out clean. Let cool for about 10 minutes; remove from the pans and cool completely on a wire rack.

To assemble the cake, place one cake layer on a serving plate. Sprinkle with brandy, if desired. Spread Cashew Crème on top of the cake layer to within ¼ inch of the edge. Place the second layer on top. Gently press it to secure it in place. Frost the entire cake with Maple Walnut Glaze.

Per serving (serves 12): Calories 510, Protein 7 g, Fat 17 g, Carbohydrate 84 g, Fiber 7 g, Sodium 522 mg

Cinnamon Apple Cake with Spiced Maple Glaze

☆ ☆

Makes one 9" round cake

This is a wonderfully easy cake that is perfect on a fall morning with a cup of chamomile tea. You can use any kind of eating apple—firm, sweet, organic if possible. Remember, the better the apples, the better the cake.

½ cup canola, safflower, or sunflower oil

½ cup maple syrup

1 cup soymilk

2 teaspoons apple cider vinegar

1 teaspoon vanilla

3½ cups barley flour

½ cup Sucanat, date sugar, or maple sugar

2 teaspoons baking soda

2 teaspoons baking powder

2 teaspoons ground cinnamon

¼ teaspoon grated nutmeg

1 teaspoon salt

4 apples, peeled, cored, and chopped

½ cup chopped walnuts (optional)

¼ cup Spiced Maple Glaze (page 110)

Maple sugar, ground cinnamon, and mint leaves

Preheat the oven to 350°F. Oil a 9" springform pan and set aside.

Mix the oil, syrup, soymilk, vinegar, and vanilla in a small bowl.

In a separate, larger bowl, mix the flour, Sucanat, baking soda, baking powder, spices, and salt.

Whisk the wet ingredients into the dry ingredients until well incorporated. Do not overwork the batter. Finish mixing with a spatula to scrape the sides of the bowl. Fold in the apples and walnuts, if desired. Pour the batter into the prepared pan.

Bake for 35 minutes and rotate the pan a half turn to ensure even baking. Bake 30 minutes more or until a knife inserted in the center comes out clean. Let cool for about 10 minutes; remove from the pan and cool completely on a wire rack.

Place the cooled cake on a wire rack over a sheet of foil or waxed paper to catch the drips. Drizzle the cake evenly with Spiced Maple Glaze. Sprinkle the top with maple sugar, cinnamon, and mint leaves.

 Per serving (serves 12): Calories 311, Protein 5 g, Fat 10 g, Carbohydrate 53 g, Fiber 7 g, Sodium 453 mg

Coconut Cake with Toasted Coconut Glaze

☆ ☆

This dessert was inspired by a a coconut cake at a wonderful restaurant in Dharamsala, India, where my friend Ravi and I began formulating its future as an incredibly delicious dessert. This cake is pretty rich, so you'll want to serve it in slightly smaller portions.

½ cup canola, safflower, or sunflower oil

½ cup maple syrup

2 cups soymilk

2 teaspoons apple cider vinegar

1 teaspoon coconut extract

1 teaspoon vanilla

½ cup maple sugar, Sucanat, or date sugar

1½ cups shredded, toasted coconut (page 101)

3½ cups barley flour

2 teaspoons baking soda

2 teaspoons baking powder

¼ teaspoon grated nutmeg

¼ teaspoon ground cinnamon

1 teaspoon salt

Preheat the oven to 350°F. Oil two 8" cake pans or one 9 x 13" pan, and set aside.

Mix the oil, syrup, soymilk, vinegar, coconut extract, and vanilla in a small bowl.

In a separate, larger bowl, mix the sugar and coconut. Sift the flour, baking soda, baking powder, spices, and salt into the coconut mixture. (Sifting isn't absolutely necessary, but it ensures there won't be clumps of flour or salt in the batter.) Whisk the wet ingredients into the dry ingredients until well incorporated. Do not overwork the batter. Finish mixing with a spatula to scrape the sides of the bowl. Pour the batter into the prepared pans.

Bake for 25 minutes; rotate the pans and continue to bake for another 10 minutes, or until a knife inserted in the center comes out clean. Let cool for about 10 minutes; remove from the pans and cool completely on a wire rack.

☆ ☆

1 recipe Toasted Coconut Glaze
   (page 114)
Extra toasted coconut and mint leaves

Place one cake layer (or the entire cake if you've baked a 9 x 13" cake) on a wire rack over a sheet of foil or waxed paper to catch the drips. Generously cover the cake layer with about 1¼ cups of the Toasted Coconut Glaze. Place the second layer on top. Gently press it to secure it in place. Drizzle the remaining glaze over the cake, beginning in the center of the top of the cake and spreading it out toward the edges with a spatula or knife so that it drips over the sides. Sprinkle with toasted coconut and mint leaves.

 Per serving (serves 16): Calories 511, Protein 6 g, Fat 29 g,
Carbohydrate 64 g, Fiber 10 g, Sodium 387 mg

Ginger-Spiced Fruit Cake with Maple Cinnamon Glaze

☆ ☆

Makes one 9" round or bundt cake or one 9 x 13" cake

This cake is delicious either with the glaze or on its own. You can choose which dried fruit you prefer to add—apples, raisins, dried pears, or all three. Nuts are also a wonderful addition to this recipe.

¼ cup canola, safflower, or sunflower oil

¼ cup maple syrup

2 tablespoons molasses

1 cup plus 1 tablespoon soymilk

1 teaspoon apple cider vinegar

1 tablespoon vanilla

¼ cup maple sugar, Sucanat, or date sugar

³⁄₄ cup diced, dried fruit: apples, pears, and raisins

1³⁄₄ cups barley flour

1 teaspoon baking soda

1 teaspoon baking powder

2 teaspoons powdered ginger

1 teaspoon ground cinnamon

¼ teaspoon ground allspice

½ teaspoon salt

⅓ cup nuts (optional)

1 recipe Spiced Maple Glaze (page 110)

Powdered maple sugar and ground cinnamon

Preheat the oven to 350°F. Oil a 9" springform or bundt cake pan or a 9 x 13" cake pan, and set aside.

Mix the oil, syrup, molasses, soymilk, vinegar, and vanilla in a small bowl.

In a separate, larger bowl, place the sugar and dried fruit; stir to coat the fruit pieces. Sift the flour, baking soda, baking powder, spices, and salt into the dried fruit-sugar mixture. (Sifting isn't absolutely necessary, but it ensures there won't be clumps of flour or salt in the batter.) Whisk the wet ingredients into the dry ingredients until well incorporated. Do not overwork the batter. Finish mixing with a spatula to scrape the sides of the bowl. Fold in the nuts. Pour the batter into the prepared pan.

Bake for 30 minutes and rotate the pan to ensure even baking. Bake 15 minutes more or until a knife inserted in the center comes out clean. Let cool for about 10 minutes; remove from the pan and cool completely on a wire rack.

Drizzle the Spiced Maple Glaze over the top of the cake, allowing it to drip evenly down the sides. Dust the top with powdered maple sugar and ground cinnamon. Serve the remaining glaze on the side.

Per serving (serves 12): Calories 299, Protein 3 g, Fat 5 g, Carbohydrate 64 g, Fiber 4 g, Sodium 277 mg

Crèmes, Frostings, and Glazes

Roasting & Toasting Nuts & Seeds

The recipes in this chapter rely on roasted nuts to bring out the rich, full flavors in these dairy-free delights. The buttery quality of the nuts makes for full-bodied crèmes that one would never know to be dairy-free. They are a delight in several of our desserts and cakes and always make a wonderful addition to any simple treat.

The following is everything you need to know to get you started roasting and toasting.

Note: Because nuts are so high in fat, they burn easily, so keep an eye on them throughout the roasting and toasting.

* Nuts with a decent amount of fat, such as cashews, almonds, walnuts, and peanuts, take well to roasting. Other nuts and seeds, such as pecans, sesame seeds, hemp nut seeds, and coconut, should be toasted on the stovetop because they can burn quickly and have to be watched carefully.

* Roasting normally occurs in a 350°F. oven. Place the nuts in a roaster pan or baking sheet, and roast until they are well browned. Stir them once or twice during the roasting process to prevent burning and to ensure an even roast.

* On the stovetop, toast nuts and seeds in a stainless steel or iron skillet over medium-low heat, stirring constantly, until they are browned and aromatic.

* Remove roasted or toasted nuts and seeds from their pans immediately so that they don't continue to cook and possibly burn. This would give them a bitter taste and render them useless.

Following are instructions for roasting or toasting the nuts and seeds used in recipes in this chapter and throughout the book.

☆ ☆

Roasting Almonds, Cashews, Hazelnuts, Peanuts, and Walnuts

Preheat the oven to 350°F. Place the almonds or pecans on a parchment-lined baking sheet or on a pan lined with a Silpat (page 120). Bake 12 to 15 minutes for almonds and walnuts—10 to 12 minutes for cashews and peanuts—or until they become aromatic. Let cool completely, at least 10 minutes.

Toasting Coconut, Hemp Nut Seeds, Pecans, and Sesame Seeds

You can pan-toast these on the stovetop over medium heat until they begin to pop and become aromatic. We suggest using a pot with sides so that when they begin to jump, they don't jump right out of your pan! Let cool completely, at least 10 minutes.

For nuts with skins

To remove the skins after roasting or toasting, gather all of the nuts in a clean dish towel, and rub the warm nuts together. (I learned this trick from Julia Child.) The skins should slip off and stay in the towel.

Blanching Almonds

Begin boiling a pot of water on the stovetop. While waiting for the water to come to a boil, prepare an ice bath for chilling the almonds after boiling by filling a large bowl with water and ice cubes; set aside. (This will keep the boiled almonds from heating further and cause the skins to separate from the almonds more easily.)

Carefully place the almonds into the boiling water, and keep at a hard boil for 5 to 6 minutes. With a slotted spoon or strainer, lift out the almonds and place them immediately into the ice bath. Wait about 15 to 30 seconds before removing. The almonds should slip out of their skins easily. If they don't, return them to the boiling water for another couple of minutes, then give them another ice bath.

Almond Crème

☆ ☆

I got this recipe from Jenny Mathau at The Natural Gourmet Cookery School in New York City. It is a sweet and lovely crème that's especially wonderful in fresh fruit tarts and in many other different desserts.

Almond Milk:

1 cup roasted almonds or blanched almonds (page 101)

2 cups water

¼ teaspoon vanilla

1 teaspoon maple syrup

Pinch of salt (optional)

Crème:

1½ tablespoons agar flakes

4 tablespoons water, divided

1 tablespoon kudzu

2 cups Almond Milk (above)

3½ tablespoons maple syrup

Pinch of salt

2 teaspoons vanilla

1 teaspoon almond extract

½ tablespoon brandy or liqueur (optional)

To make the almond milk: Process the almonds in a blender for 15 to 20 seconds. With the blender running, add the rest of the ingredients through the top; let the blender run 30 to 45 seconds more, until you have a rich, milky mixture. Strain the mixture through a sieve or a fine mesh strainer. (The milk will keep for 5 to 7 days in the refrigerator; it may settle upon standing and may need to be re-blended.)

Mix the agar in a cup with 2 tablespoons of the water. In a separate cup, dissolve the kudzu with the remaining 2 tablespoons water. Set both aside for 2 to 3 minutes.

To make the Almond Crème: In a medium saucepan over low to medium heat, cook the Almond Milk, agar mixture, syrup, and salt until the agar dissolves, 15 to 20 minutes, stirring occasionally.

Add the kudzu mixture and cook 3 to 5 minutes more, stirring constantly until the mixture begins to thicken. (If not cooked enough, the crème will maintain a starchy, chalky flavor, so don't rush this step over high heat.) Pour the mixture into a blender; add the vanilla, almond extract, and liqueur, if desired.

Caution: Blending hot liquids can be extremely dangerous. Fill the blender only halfway and proceed in batches if necessary.

☆ ☆

Blend until the mixture is smooth and well combined, about 30 to 45 seconds.

Strain through a sieve or a fine mesh strainer into a shallow dish. Cool at least 4 to 5 hours.

Note: The mixture may need to be re-blended before using. If you use a blender, the consistency will be like heavy cream. If you use a whisk, it will maintain a thicker consistency, good for tarts and crème accompaniments.

For Hazelnut Crème

Substitute hazelnuts for the almonds in the milk recipe. Use 1 teaspoon vanilla in the crème recipe.

For Mocha Crème

Add 1 tablespoon coffee substitute powder or granules and 1½ tablespoons cocoa powder to the hot mixture when it goes into the blender. Add 1 teaspoon coffee extract with the vanilla.

For Orange-Almond Crème

Substitute ¾ cup fresh orange juice for 1 cup water in the Almond Milk recipe. in the crème recipe, substitute ½ teaspoon Grand Marnier or Cointreau for the flavoring extract.

For Lemon Crème

Omit the almond extract and add 2 teaspoons lemon extract or 1 tablespoon lemon powder, and ½ tablespoon liqueur (optional).

Per serving: Calories 96, Protein 3 g, Fat 7 g,
Carbohydrate 8 g, Fiber 2 g, Sodium 3 mg

Chocolate or Carob Mousse

☆ ☆

*Makes about 4 cups
(12 servings)*

This dessert is amazing. It is just an incredible dessert, simply decadent, absolutely rich, by itself or as accompaniment to fresh fruit. We also pipe this mousse in between the layers of our Decadent Carob or Chocolate Mousse Cake (page 90).

Cashew Milk:

³/₄ cup roasted cashew pieces

2 cups water

1 teaspoon vanilla

Pinch of salt

Filling:

1¹/₂ teaspoons agar flakes

2 tablespoons water

2 cups Cashew Milk (above)

1 cup chocolate chips or vegan carob chips

1 tablespoon maple syrup

¹/₄ teaspoon salt

1 tablespoon vanilla

Process the cashews in a blender for 15 to 20 seconds. With the blender running, add the remaining ingredients through the top; let the blender run 30 to 45 seconds more, until you have a rich, milky mixture. Strain the mixture through a sieve or a fine mesh strainer. (This will keep up to 1 week in the refrigerator; it may settle upon standing and may need to be re-blended.)

Mix the agar in a cup with 2 tablespoons of the water; set aside for 5 minutes.

In a medium saucepan over low to medium heat, cook the Cashew Milk and the agar mixture until the agar dissolves, stirring occasionally, 10 to 15 minutes.

Add the chips, syrup, and salt, and cook over low heat 4 to 5 minutes more, stirring constantly until the chips are melted and the mixture looks creamy and full-bodied. Pour the mixture into a blender.

Caution: Blending hot liquids can be extremely dangerous. Fill the blender only halfway and proceed in batches if necessary.

Blend until the mixture is smooth and well combined, about 30 to 45 seconds. Blend in the vanilla, and adjust the seasonings to taste.

Strain the filling through a very fine mesh strainer or a sieve lined with cheesecloth into a large serving bowl or into individual serving dishes. Cool for at least 5 to 6 hours or overnight if possible. Serve with a nut crème and fresh berries.

Per serving: Calories 135, Protein 2 g, Fat 8 g,
Carbohydrate 14 g, Fiber 0.6 g, Sodium 46 mg

Carob or Chocolate Tofu Crème Filling

☆ ☆

Makes about 3 cups
(12 servings)

This is a wonderfully rich and creamy filling for cakes. If you love carob, this makes a wonderful filling or crème accompaniment.

16 ounces firm or extra-firm tofu

2 cups vegan carob or chocolate chips

1 cup soymilk or Cashew Milk (previous page)

1 tablespoon hot water

1 tablespoon maple syrup

1 tablespoon vanilla

⅛ teaspoon salt

In a pot of boiling water, blanch the tofu for 5 minutes; drain. (Blanching removes the bean-y flavor and results in a creamier texture.) Break up the tofu into chunks, and process in a food processor or blender for about 5 minutes. (This helps remove the gritty texture from the tofu and allows for a really smooth cream.)

Melt the carob chips in the top of a double boiler or in a bowl over a pan of boiling water. Add the melted carob and all of the remaining ingredients to the food processor or blender with the tofu. Process until all of the ingredients are well incorporated, occasionally scraping down the sides of the bowl with a spatula. When the mixture is completely smooth, transfer it to a shallow dish. Refrigerate at least 4 to 5 hours until the mixture has set up and become firm.

 Per serving: Calories 148, Protein 8 g, Fat 8 g, Carbohydrate 13 g, Fiber 1 g, Sodium 31 mg

Cashew Crème

☆ ☆

Makes about 2½ cups
(12 servings)

At Simple Treats Bakery, we use this crème for a variety of different cakes. Cashews are very rich and buttery, and they create a mild, sweet-tasting crème filled with body and richness.

1½ tablespoons agar flakes

4 tablespoons water, divided

1 tablespoon kudzu, dissolved

2 cups Cashew Milk (page 104)

3½ tablespoons maple syrup

Pinch of salt

2 teaspoons vanilla extract

½ teaspoon flavored extract, brandy, or liqueur

Mix the agar in a cup with 2 tablespoons of the water. In a separate cup, dissolve the kudzu with the remaining 2 tablespoons of water. Set both aside for 2 to 3 minutes.

In a medium saucepan over low to medium heat, cook the Cashew Milk, agar mixture, syrup, and salt for 15 to 20 minutes, stirring occasionally. Add the kudzu mixture and cook 3 to 5 minutes more, stirring constantly until the mixture begins to thicken. (If not cooked enough, the crème will maintain a starchy, chalky flavor, so don't rush this step over high heat.) Pour the mixture into a blender; add the vanilla and flavored extract.

Caution: Blending hot liquids can be extremely dangerous. Fill the blender only halfway and proceed in batches if necessary.

Blend until the mixture is smooth and well combined, about 30 to 45 seconds.

Pour into a shallow dish and refrigerate 4 to 5 hours or overnight if possible. Serve with a nut crème and fresh berries.

Note: The mixture may need to be re-blended before using. If you use a blender, the consistency will be like heavy cream. If you use a whisk, it will maintain a thicker consistency, good for tarts and crème accompaniments.

  Per serving: Calories 48, Protein 1 g, Fat 2 g, Carbohydrate 7 g, Fiber 0.4 g, Sodium 26 mg

Coffee Crème

☆ ☆

This crème is delicious between the layers of our Mocha Cake (page 83). It is also a splendid accompaniment to the Vanilla Spice Cake (page 74) with a little chocolate sauce.

1½ tablespoons agar flakes

4 tablespoons water, divided

1 tablespoon kudzu

2 cups Almond Milk (page 102)

¼ cup coffee substitute powder or granules

3½ tablespoons maple syrup

Pinch of salt

2 teaspoons coffee extract

1 teaspoon vanilla

1 teaspoon coffee-flavored liqueur

Mix the agar in a cup with 2 tablespoons of the water. In a separate cup, dissolve the kudzu with the remaining 2 tablespoons water. Set both aside for 2 to 3 minutes.

In a medium saucepan over low to medium heat, cook the Almond Milk, coffee substitute, agar mixture, syrup, and salt for 15 to 20 minutes, stirring occasionally.

Add the kudzu mixture and cook 3 to 5 minutes more, stirring constantly until the mixture begins to thicken. (If not cooked enough, the crème will maintain a starchy, chalky flavor, so don't rush this step over high heat.) Pour the mixture into a blender; add the coffee extract, vanilla, and liqueur.

Caution: Blending hot liquids can be extremely dangerous. Fill the blender only halfway and proceed in batches if necessary.

Blend until the mixture is smooth and well combined, about 30 to 45 seconds.

Pour the mixture through a sieve or a fine mesh strainer into a shallow dish. Refrigerate at least 4 to 5 hours or overnight.

Note: The mixture may need to be re-blended before using. If you use a blender, the consistency will be like heavy cream. If you use a whisk, it will maintain a thicker consistency, good for tarts and crème accompaniments.

 Per serving: Calories 103, Protein 3 g, Fat 7 g, Carbohydrate 9 g, Fiber 2 g, Sodium 4 mg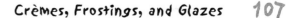

Easy Cashew Crème

☆ ☆

Wonderfully rich-tasting crème doesn't get any easier than this. Instant gratification in less than 5 minutes, and it tastes amazing. It gets thicker as it sits in the fridge, so if you like a thicker crème, allow it some time to chill. This crème is good in any cake, on top of any fruit, or on the side as a whipped cream substitute.

1 cup roasted cashews (page 101)

1 cup maple sugar, Sucanat, or date sugar

¾ cup water

1 tablespoon canola, sunflower, or safflower oil

1 teaspoon vanilla

¼ teaspoon salt

Process the cashews and sugar in a blender for 20 to 30 seconds. With the blender running, add the remaining ingredients through the top and blend for 30 to 45 seconds more. Strain through a sieve or a fine mesh strainer. Chill.

For Easy Pecan Crème

Substitute 2 cups roasted pecans for the cashews, and increase the vanilla to 2 teaspoons.

Per serving: Calories 215, Protein 4 g, Fat 13 g,
Carbohydrate 25 g, Fiber 0.8 g, Sodium 48 mg

Tofu Cashew Crème

☆ ☆

Makes 3½ cups
(12 servings)

At Simple Treats Bakery, we use this cream for a variety of different cakes, including our Strawberry Shortcake. Cashews are an extremely rich nut and make this crème heavenly. Tofu acts as a binder and a thickening agent, while the oil gives the crème sheen.

1½ tablespoons agar flakes

2 tablespoons water

2 cups Cashew Milk (page 104)

3 tablespoons maple syrup

Pinch of salt

8 ounces firm tofu, blanched (see Note)

1 tablespoon canola, sunflower, or safflower oil

½ cup maple sugar, Sucanat, or date sugar

1 tablespoon vanilla

Mix the agar in a cup with the water; set aside for 2 to 3 minutes.

In a medium saucepan over low to medium heat, cook the Cashew Milk, agar mixture, syrup, and salt 15 to 20 minutes, stirring occasionally. Pour the mixture into a blender. Add the tofu, oil, sugar, and vanilla.

Caution: Blending hot liquids can be extremely dangerous. Fill the blender only halfway and proceed in batches if necessary.

Blend until the mixture is smooth and well combined, about 50 to 60 seconds.

Pour into a shallow dish, and refrigerate at least 4 to 5 hours or overnight.

The mixture may need to be re-blended before using. If using a blender, the consistency will be like heavy cream. If using a whisk, it will maintain a thicker consistency, good for tarts and crème accompaniments.

Note: Blanch tofu by boiling in a pot of water about 5 minutes; drain. Blanching removes the bean-y flavor and results in a creamier texture.

Per serving: Calories 111, Protein 4 g, Fat 5 g, Carbohydrate 14 g, Fiber 0.8 g, Sodium 27 mg

Maple Glaze

☆ ☆

Makes about 2½ cups
(12 servings)

We use this basic glaze and the exciting variations for many of our special treats.

2 cups maple sugar, sifted
¼ teaspoon salt
¼ cup soymilk
2 teaspoons vanilla

In a small bowl, combine the sugar and salt. In a separate small bowl, combine the soymilk and vanilla.

Drizzle the soymilk mixture into the sugar mixture and stir. The consistency should be thick, smooth, and syrupy (it should coat the back of a spoon).

For Spiced Maple Glaze

Add 1 teaspoon ground cinnamon, ¼ teaspoon ground allspice, and a pinch of grated nutmeg.

For Raspberry Maple Glaze

Add 1 teaspoon almond extract and ½ cup raspberry jam.

For Maple Walnut Glaze

Add ½ cup chopped, toasted walnuts.

Per serving: Calories 123, Protein 0 g, Fat 0 g,
Carbohydrate 32 g, Fiber 0.1 g, Sodium 45 mg

Chocolate or Carob Tofu Crème Frosting

☆ ☆

Makes about 2½ cups
(12 servings)

This is the frosting we call for in many of our cakes; it's a good, basic recipe with many uses.

16 ounces firm or extra-firm tofu

2 cups chocolate chips or vegan carob chips

½ cup soymilk, almond milk (page 102), or cashew milk (page 104)

2 tablespoons coffee substitute powder or granules

⅛ teaspoon salt

1 tablespoon vanilla

1 tablespoon maple syrup

In a pot of boiling water, blanch the tofu for 5 to 7 minutes; drain. (Blanching removes the bean-y flavor and results in a creamier texture.) Process in a food processor or blender for 1 minute while tofu is still warm.

Meanwhile, melt the chips in the top of a double boiler or in a metal bowl over a pot of boiling water. (Note: Be careful to keep moisture out of the chocolate to prevent seizing, in which the chocolate becomes a solid, grainy mass that will not melt. If desired, place a bowl with the chips over the cooking tofu so that the heat from the tofu melts the chocolate.)

Add the melted chocolate, soymilk, coffee substitute, and salt to the processed tofu. Process 2 minutes more. Add the vanilla and syrup; scrape down the sides of the processor, and process briefly to incorporate.

Refrigerate at least 5 hours or overnight. Bring to room temperature before using.

Per serving: Calories 214, Protein 8 g, Fat 11 g, Carbohydrate 21 g, Fiber 1 g, Sodium 28 mg

Carob or Chocolate Ganache

☆ ☆

Makes about 2½ cups
(12 servings)

Ganache adds so much panache to cakes and baked desserts. Experiment with other ways to use it.

¼ cup coffee substitute powder or granules

2 tablespoons hot water

2 cups vegan carob chips or chocolate chips

½ cup soymilk

3 tablespoons maple syrup

¼ teaspoon salt

1 teaspoon vanilla

Dissolve the coffee substitute in the hot water in a small bowl; set aside. Melt the carob chips in the top of a double boiler.

Process the melted chips, soymilk, coffee, syrup, and salt in a food processor or blender for 2 minutes. Add the vanilla and process briefly.

Note: The ganache will set quickly as it cools, so use immediately. Cakes and cupcakes should be completely cooled before you make the ganache. To re-use or re-heat, simply warm the ganache over a double boiler until it becomes the desired consistency.

Note: If using chocolate chips, be careful to keep moisture out of the chocolate while melting. Moisture causes the chocolate to seize, in which the chocolate becomes a solid, grainy mass that will not melt.

Per serving: Calories 170, Protein 2 g, Fat 8 g, Carbohydrate 22 g, Fiber 0.5 g, Sodium 46 mg

Lemon Glaze

☆ ☆

Makes about 2½ cups

Lemon desserts are so refreshing—a perfect blend of sweetness and tartness. Use this glaze to bring a pleasantly surprising contrast to ordinary sweets.

2 cups maple sugar, Sucanat, or date sugar, sifted
⅛ teaspoon salt
Juice of 1 lemon (about ¼ cup)
2 tablespoons soymilk
2 teaspoons vanilla

Mix the sugar and salt in a small bowl. In a separate small bowl, mix the juice, soymilk, and vanilla. Drizzle the soymilk mixture into the sugar mixture and stir. The consistency should be thick, smooth, and syrupy (it should coat the back of a spoon).

  Per serving: Calories 123, Protein 0 g, Fat 0 g, Carbohydrate 33 g, Fiber 0.1 g, Sodium 23 mg

Toasted Coconut Glaze

☆ ☆

Toasting the coconut really brings out the nuttiness.

2 cups maple sugar, Sucanat, or date sugar, sifted

3/4 cup toasted, shredded coconut (page 101)

1/4 teaspoon salt

1/4 cup soymilk

1 teaspoon vanilla

1 teaspoon coconut extract

Mix the sugar, coconut, and salt in a small bowl. In a separate small bowl, mix the soymilk, vanilla, and coconut extract. Drizzle the soymilk mixture into the sugar mixture and stir. The consistency should be thick, smooth, and syrupy (it should coat the back of a spoon).

Per serving: Calories 216, Protein 1 g, Fat 1 g, Carbohydrate 36 g, Fiber 2 g, Sodium 50 mg

"Love all God's creatures, the animals, the plants, love
everything to perceive the divine mystery in all."
— Fyodor Dostoevsky

"To Believe in Love, to believe in Loveliness,
to believe in Belief."
— Shelley

"All beings tremble before violence. All fear death.
All love life. See yourself in others.
Then whom can you hurt?
What harm can you do?"
— Buddha

The Well-Stocked Vegan Baking Pantry

EVERYDAY BASICS

These are just a few of the items we recommend you have on hand in your pantry (the organic varieties, of course).

Cupboard

Apple cider vinegar
Baking soda
Baking powder
Barley flour
Barley malt syrup
Brown rice syrup
Canola, sunflower, or safflower oil
Carob and chocolate chips
Carob powder (lightly roasted)
Cocoa powder
Extracts: vanilla, coffee, raspberry, lemon, peppermint
Fruit jams: apricot, blueberry, strawberry, raspberry
Maple syrup
Peanut butter
Rolled oats
Sea salt
Soymilk (shelf-stable)
Sucanat

Refrigerator Items

Soymilk

Nuts

Almonds
Walnuts

Spices (Ground)

Allspice
Cinnamon
Cloves
Ginger (fresh and powdered)
Nutmeg (grated)

Fresh Fruit

Apples
Bananas
Pears

Dried Fruits

Raisins

Frozen Fruit

Blueberries
Raspberries

ADDITIONAL INGREDIENTS

The following is a list of ingredients that are always good to
have on hand but are not crucial.

Cupboard

Agar
Agave
Amaranth Flour
Brown rice flour
Coconut (shredded)
Coffee substitute powder or
    granules
Cornmeal
Date sugar
Kudzu
Lemon powder
Liqueurs: Cointreau, Grand
    Marnier, Kahlúa, brandy
Maple sugar or powder
Molasses

Refrigerator Items

Soymilk
Tofu, firm or extra-firm

Nuts and Seeds

Cashews
Hazelnuts
Macadamia nuts
Peanuts
Pecans
Poppy seeds
Sesame seeds

Fresh Produce

Blueberries
Lemons
Oranges
Pears
Pumpkin
Raspberries
Strawberries
Sweet potatoes

Dried Fruits

Cranberries
Dates
Raisins

Frozen Fruit

Cherries
Cranberries
Peaches
Strawberries

Spices (Ground)

Cardamom
Cloves
Ginger

Tools for the Baker

A list of the basics every kitchen needs for baking

Citrus reamer	Used to juice lemons, oranges, and other citrus fruits. We use the small, wooden ones.
Dry measures	Stackable measuring cups that range from ¼ cup to 1 cup. Use these measures for dry ingredients such as flour, dry sweeteners, powders, chopped fruits, or anything for which you need an exact measure.
Fine mesh colander	The fine mesh allows less to move through it, which is important when straining nut milks or finished crémes and glazes.
Food processor or blender	These machines are invaluable for chopping ingredients such as oats, nuts, fruits, and vegetables, and for combining and blending ingredients for nut milks, frostings, and crème fillings.
Liquid measures	Measuring cups, usually glass, with a pour spout, reserved for liquids only. Dry measurements in a liquid measure will not be accurate.
Microplane zester	One of my favorite tools. It shaves the zest from the outside of the citrus fruit, but, unlike a traditional zester, it manages to shave off three times the amount of zest. It is a wonderful tool; available at www.thegadgetsource.com.

Parchment paper	Baking paper used to line baking pans and cookie sheets to prevent sticking. Foods literally slide off parchment paper, and cleanup is about nil. Parchment paper is sold on rolls similar to waxed paper and aluminum foil and is sold in that section of the grocery store.
Pastry brush	We use this to oil baking pans. Although a clean cloth would also work well, a brush evenly distributes a fine coat of oil, creating a nonstick surface without loads of additional fat.
Pots and pans	We prefer all of our cookware to be made from stainless steel, a nonreactive metal, when at all possible. Cake pans and molds, loaf pans, and muffin tins of all shapes and sizes are available where cookware is sold. We brush a light coating of oil over the pans to create a nonstick surface and avoid the use of Teflon.
Stainless steel ice cream scoop	We use 1-ounce (about 1 heaping tablespoon) ice cream scoops for scooping cookie dough. The scoop makes easy work out of creating even and consistent cookies. If scoops are unavailable, two spoons will always do the work.
Sifters	Sifters specific to baking are available in cooking and baking supply stores, but we find a fine mesh colander will work just as well. We use them to sift dry ingredients together before mixing. Sifting separates the particles of flour, baking powder and soda, and salt to ensure a light batter without clumps or foreign matter.

Silpats	These silicone sheets are made to replace parchment traditionally used to line cookie sheets and cake pans. They are an incredible invention and a must in the serious baker's kitchen. They make for even baking, a nonstick baking surface, easy clean-up, and best of all, they are reusable thousands of times. They are temperature-safe from 40°F to over 550°F. You can order them online at www.thegadgetsource.com.
Spatulas	Used for mixing cookie batter, for the final mixing of cakes, muffins, and breads, and for folding in ingredients. Spatulas should be flexible and durable; heatproof also is an advantage.
Timer	It is important to follow the times for each recipe. Use a timer and take out the guesswork.
Whisks	Used in the mixing of batters, it aerates as you mix, resulting in a light and fluffy batter. Used for cake, muffin, and bread batters.

Sources for Ingredients & Equipment

Cuisinart Customer Service
www.cuisinart.com
150 Milford Rd.
East Windsor, NJ 08520
800-726-0190
www.theGadgetSource.com

> For Silpats, cookie scoops, whisks, spatulas, etc.

Surfas
8825 National Blvd.
Culver City, CA 90232
310-559-4770

> A baker's paradise. Surfas isn't exactly a mail-order business, but if you call and tell them what you need, they will ship it to you. They have everything—cookie sheets, loaf, cake, muffin, and brownie pans.

MAIL ORDER FOOD AND SUPPLIES AND OTHER RESOURCES

Arrowhead Mills, Inc.
P.O. Box 2059
Hereford, TX 79045
800-858-4308

> Source for barley flour and other organic ingredients

Coombs Vermont Gourmet
P.O. Box 57
Springfield, VT 05156
888-266-6271
www.maplesource.com

> Organic maple syrup and powdered maple sugar

Frontier Herbs
3021 78th St. / P.O. Box 299
Norway, IA 52318
800-786-1388

> Organic spices and herbs

Mail Order Catalog
P.O. Box 180
Summertown, TN 38483
800-695-2241
www.healthy-eating.com
email: askus@healthy-eating.com

> Vegan and organic products, Specialty, organic, and wheat-free flours (rye, barley, spelt), natural sweeteners (including stevia), Spectrum oils, Sunspire baking chips, other baking ingredients

Ojai Organics
P.O. Box 1829
Ojai, CA 93024
805-646-5759
email: Ingredients@OjaiOrganics.com
 Source for lemon powder

Pangea Vegan Products
2381 Lewis Ave.
Rockville, MD 20851
800-340-1200
www.veganstore.com
 Incredible resource for anything vegan

Spectrum Organic Products, Inc.
1304 South Point Blvd. Suite 280
Petaluma, CA 94954
707-778-8900
email: info@SpectrumOrganic.com
 Organic oils for baking

Sunspire
2114 Adams Ave.
San Leandro, CA 94577
510-569-9731
 Real vegan chocolate chips. Sunspire also sells organic dark chocolate chips as well as vegan carob chips.

Index

A

agar 17
agave syrup 16, 17
Almond
    blanching and toasting 100-01
    Butter Cookies 57
    Cornmeal Sandies 55
    Crème 102-03
    Jam Dots, Wheat-Free 46
    milk, making 102
    Ring Cake 93
    Shortbread Cookies 48
Apple
    Cake, Cinnamon 95
    Cranberry Crisp 88
    Raisin Mufins 22
    Walnut Muffins 22

B

Baked Apple-Cranberry Crisp 88
baking pans, substituting 12
baking tools 118-20
Banana Carob Chip Bread 31
Banana Nut Bread 30
barley flour 13, 17
    substituting whole wheat flour for 13
barley malt 17
barley malt syrup 16
bars
    Brown Rice Krispy Treats 72
    Chocolate Chip Blondies 71
    Double Fudge Pecan Brownies 56
Berry Cake 74
Berry Coconut Cake 80
Berry Muffins 26
Black Cherry Cake, Chocolate Chip 91
blanching almonds 101
Blondies, Chocolate Chip 71
Blueberry
    Corn Muffins 24
    Crumb Cake 89
    Muffins 20
    Oat Bran Muffins 20
    Scones 29

breads
    tips for baking 12
breads, quick
    Cornbread 33
breads, sweet
    Banana Carob Chip 31
    Banana Nut 30
    Carrot, Low-Fat 32
    Carrot Nut 32
    Chocolate Chip 35
    Cranberry Walnut 43
    Date Nut 44
    Fig-Walnut 39
    Ginger-Pear Spice 37
    Gingerbread 38
    Lemon Poppy Tea 34
    Pumpkin Spice 36
    Raspberry Lime 40
    Sweet Potato-Pecan 41
    Zucchini 42
Brown Rice Krispy Treats 72
brown rice syrup 17
Brownies, Double Fudge Pecan 56

C

Cake L'Orange 87
cakes. *See also* cakes, chocolate; cakes,
    chocolate chip
    Almond Ring 93
    Berry 74
    Berry Coconut 80
    Blueberry Crumb 89
    Cake L'Orange 87
    Carob 77
    Carob Mousse 90
    Carrot 94
    Cinnamon Apple 95
    Coconut 96-97
    Crumb 89
    Ginger-Spiced Fruit 98
    Lemon 84
    Marble Pound 78-79
    Mocha 83
    Orange 86

cakes, continued
    Peanut Butter 81
    Pineapple Crumb 89
    Raspberry-Filled Lemon 85
    Raspberry-Filled Vanilla 75
    Strawberry Shortcake 76
    tips for baking 11-12
    Vanilla Spice 74
    Vanilla, Basic 74
cakes, chocolate
    Basic 77
    Coconut 80
    Cremesicle 75
    Mousse 90
    Peanut Butter 82
    Raspberry 92
cakes, chocolate chip
    basic 74
    Black Cherry 91
    Coconut 80
    Peanut Butter 81
canola oil 13
carob 17
    Brownies 56
    Cake 77
    Coconut Chews 63
    Double Fudge Brownies 56
    Ganache 112
    Macadamia Nut Cookies 66
    Mousse 104
    Mousse Cake 90
    Tofu Crème Filling 105
    Tofu Crème Frosting 111
    Walnut Cookies, Mint 51
carob chips
    Banana Bread 31
    Blondies 71
    Cookies 68-69
Carrot Bread, Low-Fat 32
Carrot Cake 94
Carrot Nut Bread 32
Cashew
    Butter Cookies 57
    Crème 106
    Crème, Easy 108
    Jam Bites 49
    milk, making 106
    roasting 100-01
    Sandies 54

Chocolate Chip
    Black Cherry Cake 91
    Blondies 71
    Cake 74
    Coconut Cake 80
    Cookies 68
    Cookies, Oatmeal 50
    Cookies, Soy Nut Butter 65
    Cookies, Tahini 64
    Hemp Nut Seed Cookies 69
    Loaf 35
    Peanut Butter Cake 81
    Scones 29
Chocolate
    Cake 77
    Chews, Coconut 63
    Coconut Cake 80
    Crème Filling 52
    Crèmesicle Cake 75
    Ganache 112
    Macadamia Nut Cookies 66-67
    Mousse 104
    Mousse Cake 90
    Peanut Butter Cake 82
    Peanut Butter Fudge Cookies 70
    Raspberry Cake 92
    Spiral Cookies 52-53
    Tofu Crème Frosting 111
    Tofu Crème Filling 105
    Walnut Cookies, Mint Double 51
Cinnamon Apple Cake 95
Cinnamon-Maple Sugar 22
Cinnamon Snaps 60
Clove Cookies 58
Coconut
    Cake 96
    Cake, Berry 80
    Cake, Chocolate 80
    Cake, Chocolate Chip 80
    Chocolate Chews 63
    Glaze, Toasted 114
    Macaroons 62
    toasting 63, 100-01
Coffee Crème 107
coffee substitutes 17
cookies
    Almond Butter 57
    Almond Jam Dots 46
    Almond Shortbread 48

cookies, continued
    Cashew Butter 57
    Cashew Jam Bites 49
    Chocolate Chip 68
    Chocolate-Chocolate Macadamia Nut 66
    Chocolate Peanut Butter Fudge 70
    Chocolate Spiral 52-53
    Chocolate Walnut, Mint Double 51
    Cinnamon Snaps 60
    Clove 58
    Coconut Chocolate Chews 63
    Coconut Macaroons 62
    Cornmeal Sandies 55
    Ginger Snaps 60
    Gingerbread 61
    Hemp Nut Seed, Chocolate Chip 69
    Lemon Ginger Snaps 59
    Lemon Poppy Seed 59
    Mint Double Carob Walnut 51
    Oatmeal Chocolate Chip 50
    Oatmeal Raisin 50
    Peanut Butter & Jelly Thumbprints 47
    Sandies, Cashew or Pecan 54
    Soy Nut Butter Chocolate Chip 65
    Tahini Chocolate Chip 64
    tips for baking 11
Corn Muffins 24
Cornbread 33
Cornmeal Sandies 55
Cranberry
    Crisp, Baked Apple 88
    Orange Muffins 23
    Orange Scones 27
    Walnut Bread 43
Crème
    Almond 102-03
    Cashew 106
    Coffee 107
    Easy Cashew 108
    Filling, Carob or Chocolate Tofu 105
    Filling, Chocolate 52
    Pecan 108
    Tofu Cashew 109
Crèmesicle Cake, Chocolate 75
Crisp, Baked Apple-Cranberry 88
Crumb Cake 89

D
dates
    Coconut Macaroons 62
    Coconut Chocolate Chews 63
    Nut Bread 44
    sugar 13, 16, 17
desserts
    Baked Apple-Cranberry Crisp 88
    Mousse, Chocolate or Carob 104
Double Chocolate Peanut Butter Cake 82
Double Fudge Brownies 56

F
Fig-Walnut Bread 39
fillings
    Almond Crème 102-03
    Carob Tofu Crème 105
    Cashew Crème 106
    Cashew Crème, Easy 108
    Cashew Crème, Tofu 109
    Chocolate Creme 52
    Chocolate Tofu Crème 105
    Coffee Crème 107
    Hazelnut Crème 103
    Lemon Crème 103
    Mocha Crème 103
    Mousse, Chocolate or Carob 104
    Orange-Almond Crème 103
    Pecan Crème 108
    Tofu Cashew Crème 109
frostings. *See also* glazes
    Carob or Chocolate Ganache 112
    Chocolate or Carob Tofu
    Crème 111
Fruit Cake, Ginger-Spiced 98
Fudge Brownies 56
Fudge Cookies, Chocolate Peanut Butter 70

G
Ganache, Carob or Chocolate 112
genetically altered foods (GMO) 15
ginger
    Gingerbread 38
    Gingerbread Cookies 61
    Pear Spice Loaf 37
    Snaps 60
    Snaps, Lemon 59
    Spiced Fruit Cake 98

glazes
    Maple 110
    Lemon 113
    Toasted Coconut 114

H
Hazelnut Crème 103
Hemp Nut Seed Cookies, Chocolate Chip 69
hemp nut seeds, toasting 100-01

J
Jam Dots, Almond 46

K
kudzu 18

L
Lemon
    Cake 84
    Crème 103
    Ginger Snaps 59
    Glaze 113
    Poppy Seed Cookies 59
    Poppy Tea Bread 34
lemon powder 18
    source 18, 122
Lime Bread, Raspberry 40
Loaf, Chocolate Chip 35
Loaf, Ginger-Pear Spice 37
Low-Fat Carrot Bread 32

M
Macadamia Nut Cookies, Chocolate 66-67
Macaroons, Coconut 62
Maple
    Glaze 110
    sugar 13, 16, 18
    syrup 18
    Walnut Glaze 110
Marble Pound Cake 78-79
Mint Double Carob Walnut Cookies 51
Mint Double Fudge Brownies 56
mise en place 13
Mocha Cake 83
Mocha Crème 103
Mocha Fudge Brownies 56
Mousse, Chocolate or Carob 104
muffins
    Apple-Raisin 22
    Apple-Walnut 22
    Berry 26
    Blueberry 20

muffins, continued
    Blueberry Corn 24
    Blueberry-Oat Bran 20
    Corn 24
    Cranberry-Orange 23
    Orange Corn 24
    Peach-Oat Bran 25
    Raspberry 21
    tips for baking 12

N
nut breads
    Banana Nut 30
    Banana Carob Chip 31
    Carrot Nut 32
    Cranberry Walnut 43
    Date Nut 44
    Fig-Walnut 39
    Sweet Potato Pecan 41

O
Oat Bran Muffins, Blueberry 20
Oat Bran Muffins, Peach 25
Oatmeal Chocolate Chip Cookies 50
Oatmeal Raisin Cookies 50
oils 13
Orange
    Almond Crème 103
    Brownies, Double Fudge 56
    Cake 86
    Corn Muffins 24
    Cranberry Muffins 23
    Scones, Cranberry 27
organic foods 14-15

P
pantry list 116-18
parchment paper 119
Peach-Oat Bran Muffins 25
Peanut Butter
    Cake 81
    Cake, Chocolate 82
    Cake, Chocolate Chip 81
    Fudge Cookies, Chocolate 70
    & Jelly Thumbprints 47
Pear Spice Loaf, Ginger 37
Pecan
    Bread, Sweet Potato 41
    Cornmeal Sandies 55
    Crème 108
    Double Fudge Brownies 56

Pecan, continued
    Sandies 54
    Scones, Raisin 28
    toasting 100-01
Pineapple Crumb Cake 89
poppy seeds
    Lemon Cookies 59
    Lemon Tea Bread 34
Pound Cake, Marble 78-79
Pumpkin Spice Bread 36

Q

quick breads. *See* breads; sweet breads

R

raisins
    Apple Muffins 22
    Gingerbread 38
    Oatmeal Cookies
    Pecan Scones 28
Raspberry
    Chocolate Chip Loaf 35
    Filled Lemon Cake 85
    Filled Vanilla Cake 75
    Lime Bread 40
    Maple Glaze 110
    Muffins 21
Rice Krispy Treats, Brown 72
rice syrup 16
roasting nuts and seeds 100-01

S

safflower oil 13
Sandies, Cashew or Pecan 54
Sandies, Cornmeal 55
Scones
    Blueberry 29
    Chocolate Chip 29
    Cranberry-Orange 27
    Raisin-Pecan 28
Shortbread Cookies, Almond 48
Shortcake, Strawberry 76
sifting, about 13
Silpats 119
sources for ingredients and equipment
    121-22
soymilk 18
Soy Nut Butter Chocolate Chip Cookies 65
Spice Bread, Pumpkin 36

Spiced Maple Glaze 110
Spicy Cornbread 33
Strawberry Shortcake 76
Sucanat 13, 16, 18
sunflower oil 13
Sweet Potato-Pecan Bread 41
Sweet Potato Purée 41, 56
sweeteners
    refined 15-16
    substituting 13, 16

T

tahini 18
Tahini Chocolate Chip Cookies 64
Toasted Coconut Glaze 114
toasting nuts and seeds 100-01
Tofu Cashew Crème 109
Tofu Crème Filling, Chocolate or Carob 105
Tofu Crème Frosting, Chocolate or Carob
    111

V

Vanilla Cake
    Basic 74
    Raspberry-Filled 75
    Spice 74
vegan baking tips 11-13
veganism 14

W

Walnut
    Apple Muffins 22
    Banana Nut Bread 30
    Banana Carob Chip Bread 31
    Bread, Cranberry 43
    Bread, Fig 39
    Carrot Nut Bread 32
    Crumb Cake 89
    Date Nut Bread 44
    Mint Double Carob Cookies 51
Wheat-Free Almond Jam Dots 46
wheat-free foods 15
whole wheat pastry flour 13
    substituting barley flour for 13

Z

zest, citrus 18
Zucchini Bread 42

BOOK PUBLISHING COMPANY

since 1974—books that educate, inspire, and empower

To find your favorite vegetarian and soyfood products online, visit:

www.healthy-eating.com

Living in the Raw
Rose Lee Calabro
1-57067-148-6 $19.95

Stevia: The Natural Sweetener for Drinks, Desserts, Baked Goods and More!
Rita DePuydt
1-57067-133-8 $14.95

Dairy-Free & Delicious
Brenda Davis, R.D
recipes by Bryanna Grogan
& Joanne Stepaniak
1-57067-124-9 $12.95

The New Now & Zen Epicure
Miyoko Nishimoto Schinner
1-57067-114-1 $19.95

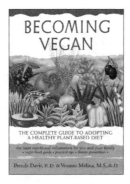

Becoming Vegan
Brenda Davis, R.D.,
Vesanto Melina, R.D.,
1-57067-103-6 $16.95

Vegan Vittles
Joanne Stepaniak
1-57067-025-0 $11.95

Purchase these health titles and cookbooks from your local bookstore or
natural food store, or you can buy them directly from:

Book Publishing Company • P.O. Box 99 • Summertown, TN 38483
1-800-695-2241

Please include $3.95 per book for shipping and handling.